ALL THINGS BEING EQUAL

ALL THINGS BEING EQUAL

THE GENESIS, COSTS, AND AFTERMATH OF THE USWNT'S EQUAL PAY BATTLE

RICH NICHOLS

WITH SAM YIP

FOREWORD BY HOPE SOLO

Skyhorse Publishing

Skyhorse Publishing books may be purchased in bulk at special discounts for sales promotion, corporate gifts, fund-raising, or educational purposes. Special editions can also be created to specifications. For details, contact the Special Sales Department, Skyhorse Publishing, 307 West 36th Street, 11th Floor, New York, NY 10018 or info@skyhorsepublishing.com.

Skyhorse® and Skyhorse Publishing® are registered trademarks of Skyhorse Publishing, Inc.®, a Delaware corporation.

Visit our website at www.skyhorsepublishing.com.
Please follow our publisher Tony Lyons on Instagram @tonylyonsisuncertain.

10 9 8 7 6 5 4 3 2 1

Library of Congress Cataloging-in-Publication Data is available on file.

Cover design by Brian Peterson
Cover photos by Getty Images

ISBN: 978-1-5107-7868-9
Ebook ISBN: 978-1-5107-7869-6

Printed in the United States of America

Contents

PART III

Author's Note

LEADERSHIP IS A costly endeavor.

Anyone choosing to lead knows that goals are defined, and outcomes are uncertain. But one thing is for sure: the journey will be painful. That's why very few people are true leaders.

Growing up, I never saw myself as a leader. However, I always knew what I wanted, knew it would require hard work to achieve my objectives, and that despite the pain of the journey, I might not achieve the goals.

In many ways, that's how I viewed, approached, and pursued the quest for equal pay with the United States Women's National Soccer Team (USWNT). It was quite plainly, the honor of a lifetime to be chosen by the women of the World Cup champion USWNT to guide them through this truly epic, historic battle for equal pay.

I never once doubted the sanctity of the objective. I never once questioned my commitment or abilities to lead the perennial Olympic and World Cup champions to secure equal pay. I never once harbored any fear of the US Soccer Federation (USSF). I never once questioned the resolve and leadership of Hope Solo, the GOAT goalkeeper, and unwavering USWNT leader in the decades long quest for equal pay.

But, from the outset, given the challenges—especially knowing that the powerful US Soccer Federation would pull out all stops to crush the drive for equal pay– I naturally wondered how long the USWNT's total, 100 percent commitment to do whatever it took to get equal pay would last.

Notwithstanding, at that time (2015) in my life and long career, after being engaged in the representation of several extremely high-profile clients embroiled in historic, media-driven, existential sports and sophisticated business scandals, I had no idea of the USWNT's true level of commitment. I had no idea how long they'd keep me around as their leader. I had no idea how long they could withstand the pressure and pain I knew the US Soccer Federation would reign down on the players individually and collectively during the equal pay journey.

But I knew the trip would be unprecedented. Accordingly, I kept a brain-based record of critical events, conversations, meetings, negotiations, telephone calls, interviews, media encounters, and other noteworthy happenings during my almost two-year ride representing the USWNT.

It was 2018 before I began to think about writing a book to chronicle the USWNT's epic journey. Specifically, when we filed Hope Solo's violation of the Equal Pay Act and Title VII lawsuit against the U.S. Soccer Federation in August 2018 and no one on the team or their lawyers responded to Hope's overtures to join the lawsuit, and the media didn't acknowledge or report on the filing of the litigation—I knew that going forward the narrative about the USWNT's quest for equal pay would change.

That's when I had my first thoughts about the need to historically chronicle and ultimately report the genesis of the explosive ingredients required to develop the once in a lifetime, dynamic, historic game-changing, USWNT "perfect storm"—a seismic phenomenon that, if superbly executed, could result in equal pay—not only for the courageous women of the 2015 World Cup champion United States Women's National Soccer Team, but for women in the world's diverse industrial workforces.

A perfect storm can be aptly described as the natural convergence of powerful environmental forces—in this instance, the powerful and indomitable USWNT personalities, leadership, an embattled time-worn, familiar and tiresome landscape, untenable circumstances, timing, ingenuity, bravery, burning desire, intuition, unspoken but palpable togetherness, humanity and above all—the diverse degrees of individual and collective resolve and capacity to execute—all came together, absent any prompting, to create the menacing USWNT thunderclouds that would produce the deafening thunderclap demands for equal pay; indeed—terrific, insistent rumblings for equality from the USWNT—that would be heard around the world.

Clearly, the ingredients and the trail blazed by the USWNT to equal pay had to be memorialized for future generations of women to emulate. Thus, the writing of this book to chronicle the intrepid USWNT journey slowly but surely began to consume me.

Importantly, when you are in the midst of a battle or ebullient journey, you tend to emblazon much of what transpires in your brain. That's what I did. I remember situations, comments made, questions asked, impressions, expressions and have the innate ability to "playback" experiences in audio and or video or audio video format.

Accordingly, the work you are about to read contains the recounting of descriptive scenarios, conversations and quoted dialogue—all of which is reported via my memory. These particular situations were powerful and impressionable enough for me to remember quite vividly.

Importantly, although the quoted discussions may not be 100 percent accurate, they are nonetheless as close to totally accurate as memory allows.

I am humbled that you have chosen to invest your valuable time to read this story, and I trust that you'll come away with nothing but unbridled affection and respect for the perennial Olympic and World Cup champion United States Women's National Soccer Team.

Foreword

Hope Solo

IN MY EARLY days on the US Women's National Soccer Team, I sensed that we as women were treated differently. I couldn't quite put my finger on exactly what it was that gave me that feeling, but I had experienced enough disrespect in my relatively young life to feel it in the air.

Being raised and influenced by two incredibly strong and intelligent women created an environment for me growing up where asking questions and educating myself was encouraged. Breaking barriers is how my grandma lived her life, and my mom knew no other way but to force men in science or martial arts to see her as their equal. So, being Alice Shaw's granddaughter and Judy's daughter, I was never shy about pointing out inequities. Shitty practice facilities, uncut, unlined, un-level fields, unkempt goals, and unsanitary locker rooms. I had the highest expectations playing on the best team in the world. I was disappointed time and time again.

Anyone who cared to look saw that the men were not training and playing at these same backwater stadiums. They weren't using the same training fields, they weren't playing as many games on turf, and they were not staying in three-star hotels. We knew the guys were flying to tournaments in chartered private flights and staying in five-star hotels. Everybody including players, coaches, staff, and the executives themselves would shrug, laugh it off, and insinuate with their smug or helpless faces, that there was nothing that could be done. Acceptance and gratitude was embedded in the US Soccer badge of approval. It meant we stay in line. Play soccer and shut up.

My teammates often bristled at my outspoken demeanor. They thought that being nice would bring benefits. That was the prevailing view.

I never bought into that perspective.

History teaches us that those in power do not relinquish it. Power must be taken. The 19th Amendment and the 15th Amendment—women's right to vote and African American men's right to vote respectively, were societal changes made by men and women who sacrificed everything to alter the course of not only history, but the path of human existence in the United States. These rights were not given because of the good graces of others. It was a bloody mess, filled with pain, tears, and sacrifice. This is how nations and society have progressed for the better throughout history.

People must stand together and realize that when they're knocked down, they must get back up and remain standing in the end until the battle is won if they want history to change. When men and women stand for something, fight for change, they must live it and believe in it, and they must be willing to mend their battle wounds. They must be willing to take hits.

How does one win in the end? When winning consists of treading lightly on those who don't have the stomach for the fight, and for those who don't have the fortitude to stare the enemy in the eye and not falter. The fight for equal pay is not for those who don't want to cause a stir, or for the faint of heart or mind, and certainly not for those whose self-interest is mired in social media fame and greed.

The undigestible truth is I'm embarrassed. How, as a woman who prides herself in knowing my rights and doing my due diligence, who was taught to question everything as a child, how is it that I found myself in a position with zero knowledge of my own lawful rights? I was ashamed and enraged to find out that the battle I was fighting for—personal dignity and respect—was actually guaranteed to me. How were none of us on the USWNT educated in the Equal Pay Act? These aren't just some words on paper. These acts, these laws are spelled out in our

Constitution. We weren't asking for new law to be written. We were demanding the Federation abide by the United States Constitution, and their response to our demands was appalling.

After all, it had been a long time since anyone else had asked these questions. Why are we flying to the Olympics in economy? Why does the men's youth team get a charter? Why are we not asking for the same travel arrangements in our contracts? These questions seemed too simple, too obvious. What I saw around me were scared faces, scared young players, scared older players. Most everybody stuck with the mantra of being grateful and happy just to be there, and thus agreeable to most of these details. The greatest obstacle was ourselves, of us getting in our own way time and time again, and abiding by the subservient culture embedded in the system that is US Soccer. The men who made the decisions we felt beholden to. How dare we upset them? We were disappointing our "daddies"—our employer.

After the 2015 World Cup, I was able to say that I accomplished my lifelong dreams and goals of being the best goalkeeper in the world, being an Olympic gold medalist, and finally being a World Cup champion. My passion for soccer in 2016 didn't burn inside me as much as this new shining ember that became a part of my soul—this ember being the desire to shift and change women's opportunities in every landscape for generations to come through our no-holds-barred battle with our employer-the magnanimous and infallible US Soccer Federation. We were backed by our Constitution, the Equal Pay Act, and Title VII. There was rumbling excitement, concern, and confusion from fans to players alike. The ultimate goal was not just to force US Soccer's hand to abide by federal law and show us the money, but also to win the fight in the courts, so that we would guarantee true equality for women. We knew the world was watching, and one of the most popular teams in the world was taking the lead for this just cause. It has been my experience that the right *people* must be put into place for a monumental fight like this to get off the ground. Our hope came to us in our first meeting with Rich Nichols. This is the moment the seed was planted.

For so long, I thought our team would continue down the same road, with the same executive director, John Langel. Blind loyalty to those who came before was another major hurdle the USWNT had to overcome. I knew we needed a tough representative willing to fearlessly challenge the US Soccer Federation.

Through a friend of a friend, we were put in touch with Rich Nichols. Rich had extensive experience in the sports industry and was known to be a smart, fearless negotiator and champion for athletes' rights. Our first meeting with Rich changed everything.

Ultimately, Rich's colleague Art McAfee, a lawyer with seventeen years of experience negotiating collective bargaining agreements as senior counsel with the NFL Players Association, joined our team. As a result, we had two seasoned Black lawyers teaching a robust group of mostly white women about our rights in the workplace. Rich and Art also schooled us about the Equal Pay Act; Title VII wage discrimination; and how our resolve, commitment, and unity would provide us the power to demand and effect changes from the US Soccer Federation.

Nichols mapped out a plan of action showing us where our strength resided and convincing us of the power we had as a collective, unified force. Importantly, Rich and Art spelled out the sacrifices we would have to make, assured us that the battle for equal pay would not be easy, but encouraged us that we could do it.

It was empowering. There was hope that with new leadership we could finally stand up to our oppressors, who had been making money off of the backs of the women's players for decades. After our first meeting with Rich, we took a vote, and once again we voted to keep our longtime executive director John Langel. We complained about contracts and the treatment by the federation, but we continued to vote for the familiarity of being treated as second-class citizens. We continued with Langel, who was apparently unwilling to broach topics like equal travel or equal pay with former president of the federation Sunil Gulati. Langel intimated to us that Gulati viewed those topics as "non-starters." Apparently, that is all my former teammates needed to be told in order to fall into line and continue down the road of silent enablers.

It took almost two years after our first meeting with Rich and two more votes before the players finally realized that the team needed change, and we had to stand for something or continue to fall for everything.

Initial intentions may have been pure, but hardships, bumps in the road, and fear can turn even the purest of intentions. Many were led astray, and one by one the house started to fall. We saw the age-old tactic of divide and conquer play out in front of our eyes, even though we knew that was US Soccer's bread and butter. It was another almost impossible challenge we had to overcome.

How are we going to stay together, when all of us are getting pulled, prodded, and infiltrated by US Soccer's agents, executives and even management consulting firms. This is what Rich warned us about. We had to find a way to stand strong together. Instead we were riddled with doubt, fear, selfishness, and a lack of iron will.

The players who were the loudest were also the ones who caved, who backed down, who settled. Our fight which should have played out in court as a road map for women creating legal precedence to refer to for all time. Instead, it played out over social media, with uninformed players, sponsors, media, and fans alike.

It took almost eight years of winning Olympic and World Cup championships, of enduring center seat air travel, staying at Motel 6–type hotel accommodations, dealing with lengthy training residencies, and expecting to be respected by the US Soccer Federation before the rest of the women on the US Women's National Soccer Team realized it wasn't going to happen and that being nice, respectful, and obedient women wasn't the way to wake the Federation up. Hoping for change was merely a pipe dream.

The full story of our fight for equal pay has never been told. It certainly wasn't a walk in the park. There are rare moments in life where the right people are in the right place at the right time. There can be no doubt that the fight for equal pay on the USWNT was birthed in our minds and hearts by a man ready to fight and stand for a greater cause. If Rich Nichols had not met with our team that fall evening in a hotel conference room, we would still be decades behind in our pursuit for equality.

This is the true accounting of our fight for equal pay on the USWNT. Rich can speak firsthand about the struggles we faced, the highs and the lows, the hope, the false hope, and the historic moments in our assault on archaic rule within US Soccer.

We never won in court. We never set legal precedent as a guiding light for other women facing gender discrimination. The USWNT's fight for equal pay and equal treatment continues. My hope is that the true telling of our fight, our successes, and our failures will serve as inspiration for those who are unwilling to accept anything but true equality.

It was the honor and privilege of a lifetime to represent the United States.

I proudly bear the scars of sacrifice in the fight for equal pay.

Thank you, Rich, for setting the wheels in motion and forever helping us change the landscape of sports in America.

May everyone have the courage and resilience to fight for change.

Prologue

"Merit Pay"

MERIT PAY. THAT'S how US Soccer board member and their lead negotiator, Donna Shalala, described the paltry $72,000 per year paid to the 2015 World Cup champion United States Women's National Soccer Team in their battle for equal pay. A $72,000 salary was to Ms. Shalala simply what the players on the US Women's National Soccer Team "merited." Essentially, that was their worth.

After the almost thirty-minute poverty presentation provided by then-US Soccer's Chief Financial Officer Eric Gleason during the first hour of the first day of our collective bargaining agreement negotiations in 2016, I asked the obligatory question.

Why did the USWNT not get paid the $292,000 per player that the US Men's National Soccer Team get paid?

"Merit pay" proclaimed Donna Shalala, sitting up in her chair as if she was just caught sleeping in class.

"Merit pay," she repeated, "the women get merit pay."

I turned and looked at USWNT counsel Art McAfee with a Scooby-Doo expression on my face. He looked at me similarly flummoxed.

Somehow, I found the words quickly to emphasize my utter perplexity. "Are you telling us that the $72,000 that the top twelve players on the women's national team are paid is merit pay? Do you mean, that's what they are worth?"

Before Ms. Shalala could respond, I continued.

"They've won perennial Olympic gold medals, three World Cup championships, and 95 percent of their matches and you're telling us that $72,000 for the Top Tier 1 players, $54,000 for Tier 2 players, and $36,000 for the Tier 3 players on this team is merit pay?"

"Are you telling us that this is what they are worth?"

"Because," I continued, "that's what merit pay is. It's the economic value of your worth depicted in dollars paid to you in compensation for the professional services you provide. That's merit pay. Is that what you're telling us, Ms. Shalala?"

"Absolutely" she said without hesitation. "Absolutely. They are getting paid based on their merit."

A pretty incredible and revealing response.

Is it so ingrained in the psyche of women that men consider them second-class citizens with a sense of value and worth determined by men?

Is that notion of "worth" so entrenched that erstwhile champions of equal pay—such as Donna Shalala, president of the Clinton Foundation and 2016 presidential candidate Hillary Clinton confidant, and Kathryn Ruemmler, President Barack Obama's White House counsel and now US Soccer's outside counsel and key "no equal pay" negotiator—can actually work to convince women like those in the USWNT that they are in fact not worth what their less successful male counterparts get paid?

Apparently, that is the case.

Shameful.

It took me a while to accept that this was the very real dynamic we faced in this battle for equal pay.

It was a painful, sobering reality.

Shalala and Ruemmler, stalwart champions of equal pay, actually believed that if the men controlling the U.S. Soccer Federation determined that the uncelebrated, unsuccessful USMNT deserved to be paid 75 percent *more* than the perennial Olympic and World Cup champion women on the USWNT and believed it to the extent that they were willing to risk their professional reputations representing the US Soccer Federation in its fight to deny the USWNT equal pay, then the USWNT were certainly about to embark upon what CBS's *60 Minutes* aptly labeled as "The Match of their Lives."

PART I

1

Genesis

IN A MID-DECEMBER 2012 team meeting, the decorated and arguably the greatest of all-time United States Women's National Team
(USWNT) goalkeeper, Hope Solo, lambasted the celebrated USWNT's
longtime counsel for being too chummy with the United States Soccer
Federation and its president and oppressor-in-chief Sunil Gulati. Solo
wanted their counsel to aggressively advocate for a substantial player
salary increase in the middle of negotiations with US Soccer for a new
collective bargaining agreement (CBA).

Solo convinced her equally perturbed teammates—comprised of a
supermajority of equally frustrated underpaid and disrespected veteran
players—that it was time for their US Women's National Team Players
Association (USWNTPA) executive director and counsel to be replaced
with a strong, tough representative who would not be afraid of the US
Soccer Federation, would not negotiate with a soft spot for management, and who would fight for the team and get them the money they
want in the new collective bargaining agreement (CBA).

At the recommendation of her financial advisor, Solo placed her
first call to me, Rich Nichols, and the real battle for equal pay began.

Importantly, in 2012, for the first time since 1999, as a result of the
huge success the team enjoyed with successive Olympic championships

and a close-call second-place finish in the 2011 World Cup, the "cycle" of older players dropping off the team for a host of reasons— most often because of the—when compared to the monies earned by professional athletes in other sports, and in this instance, the dollars paid to the comparatively unsuccessful US Men's National Soccer Team—relative poverty wages paid to the professional USWNT players— and young replacement players imbued with the effervescent, *I'm just happy to be on the USWNT, I don't care what I get paid* mentality had ended.

Now, the veterans controlled the team.

Thus, the hardened, battle-tested, experienced old guard were relatively fearless and had the leverage and courage to push beyond their usual USWNT compensation boundaries. All they needed was a strong leader.

The question: Was Nichols the right choice to represent them?

Why Me?

As I embarked upon this journey to write this book about my experiences as a champion of women's rights in sports, I've been asked by literary agents and publishers alike—why do I think I'm the right person to tell the story?

In fact, I've even been asked the question, Why do you think a Black man like yourself can tell the story about the pursuit of equality and compensation by mostly white female athletes?"

Well, I'll tell you why I'm the right person to tell the story. I'll tell you exactly why I am the *best* person to tell you about how the United States Women's National Soccer Team pursued equal pay.

The fact of the matter is I lived it. Twice.

Some even say that I've blazed some trails in the pursuit of equity and equality for women in sport. As delineated in the pages ahead, in 1995 I was privileged to have had the opportunity to be an erstwhile founder of the American Basketball League (ABL), the premier women's professional basketball league. The ABL's mission was to provide an equitable opportunity for our best female collegiate basketball players to stay home in the USA instead of venturing off to an unsafe country or corner of the world and risk their lives pursuing their dreams of being a professional, and to pay the players a minimum of $100,000 (worth about $200,000 today) per year to play professional basketball at home.

Subsequently, almost twenty years later in 2014, the World Cup and Olympic champion USWNT via Hope Solo's financial advisor secured my services to be the executive director and general counsel of the US Women's National Team Players Association (USWNTPA) to lead them in their existential battle with the United States Soccer Federation for equal pay.

Accordingly, I have amassed some pretty serious experiences in the never-ending battle for equity and equality for strong, independent, never-say-die women in sport. Thus, I am more than qualified to tell the tales that I lived.

Origins in the Early '80s

In fact, my professional journey with regard to promoting athletes' rights and challenging gargantuan international governing bodies of Olympic sport actually started way back in the late 1970s and early 1980s when I, as an 800-meter specialist and member of the United States track team, joined three other world-class athletes, the greatest of all-time, 400-meter hurdler Edwin Moses; brilliant 800-meter competitor and member of the US track team Doriane Lambelet-Coleman (who now teaches law at Duke University); and the late great Olympic gold medal sprinter Harvey Glance, in the creation of the stringent in-competition performance-enhancing drug-testing protocols in track and field that were ultimately adopted in Olympic sport.

Specifically, we wanted to level the competitive playing field against the athletes of Eastern Bloc nations (e.g. East Germany, Czechoslovakia, Soviet Union). At that time, it was well known in the international track and field community that athletes from those nations benefited from the state-supported use of steroids and other performance-enhancing drugs.

Between 1979 to 1982, the four of us and Jim Coleman, a brilliant "Big Law" employment lawyer and death penalty case specialist who was notorious serial killer Ted Bundy's last death penalty appellate lawyer, painstakingly created the toughest in-competition drug-testing protocols in Olympic sport. But to our surprise, these protocols were not easily embraced or accepted by the powers that be, which were the International Olympic Committee (IOC), US Olympic Committee (USOC), and The Athletics Congress (TAC), which is now USA Track & Field (USATF). At the time, we were young, naïve athletes, still immersed in the misguided belief that everyone wanted fairness in Olympic sports.

What we learned later is that fair and merit-based performances were actually antithetical to the real objectives of the guardians of Olympic sport. As athletes in the Free World, unbeknownst to us, we were pawns in the balancing of power and politics in international sports.

Power, politics, and economics actually controlled the business of Olympic sports, with regards to the Eastern Bloc nations' use of PEDs which guaranteed Olympic gold medals for them, and the ensuing worldwide showcase of the Olympic medal ceremony. All of this resulted in providing worldwide promotion of their people and authoritative countries and in some way balanced the equation of world power and politics on the backs of performance-enhancement drug-free athletes in the USA and other democratic nations who lost Olympic championships to their juiced competitors. This was essentially sportswashing of those times. Thus, the abject reluctance of the IOC, USOC, and TAC to embrace our revolutionary in-competition drug testing protocols.

In fact, it took a veiled threat from USA track athletes that absent in-competition drug-testing of all countries participating in the 1984 Los Angeles Olympic Games, US track athletes might boycott the LA Olympics and embarrass their own host country to convince those august international governing bodies of Olympic sport to adopt our tough in-competition drug testing protocols. Succinctly stated, we as American athletes wanted to have a fair, equal opportunity to compete for Olympic gold.

Thus, as a track and field athlete in the early 1980s, I had the admittedly harrowing experience of pushing back on the supremely powerful governing bodies of Olympic sport. Instructively, dealing with immovable, traditional, white male–controlled national governing bodies of Olympic sport prepared me for my future encounters with the entrenched, conservative, decidedly autocratic, modern-day US Soccer Federation (USSF).

Accordingly, when Hope Solo initially contacted me in December 2012 to represent the USWNT in their battles with the USSF, I fully understood the steadfast juggernaut of political and economic power that the United States Women's National Soccer Team would face in the quest for equal pay. I understood that there was going be tremendous pushback from the largely male-dominated government-like, bureaucratic, inflexible, and powerful organizations like FIFA and the United States Soccer Federation. FIFA is the world governing body of soccer and the USSF is second only to FIFA with regard to established plenary global power in the sport.

I knew that not only were these organizations going to push back hard on the *notion* that women should be paid equally in the sport of soccer, but also US Soccer and FIFA were going to fight tooth and nail to make sure equal pay remained just a notion and never became a reality.

Strong Women

I'm frequently asked why I have spent most of my career representing strong women in sports.

Why did I find myself representing strong women like the ABL's Olympic-champion founding players Marion Jones, Hope Solo, and ultimately the United States Women's National Soccer Team, comprised in part of quintessential strong women—Becky Sauerbrunn, Abby Wambach, Christie Rampone, Shannon Boxx, Lauren Holiday, Alex Morgan, Carli Lloyd, Megan Rapinoe, Sydney Leroux and others. All of the players on the USWNT were in a quest for the power to control their own destiny in what was a perennial, seemingly futile fight for respect and equality with FIFA and the United States Soccer Federation—organizations supposedly created in substantive part to champion opportunity for women.

To be honest, I'm not exactly sure why or how I found myself in what I considered to be an enviable, privileged position of working with strong women in sports. I can only think that I'm drawn to strong, independent women like my wife who are naturally willing to fight the powers that be for the right to carve out their own professional paths, earn a living wage, and sometimes passively but most times aggressively persist with the demand to be treated equally with respect, just like the men in their respective professions.

Jennie, my wife of thirty-two years, was a budding broadcast journalist when we met in 1988. I was managing a relatively complicated referendum political campaign in San Francisco. She came to interview me and we had dinner a few weeks later after the election, and we have been together ever since.

Jennie is a strong, no-nonsense, calls it like she sees it, independent, whip-smart, intuitive, passively aggressive woman. In other words, she is well equipped to keep me in check. She loves journalism, but she didn't love it enough to compromise her gender and self-respect to stay in the business. After being told what type of clothes to wear, how to style her hair, and how to write her own copy to be delivered in roadside stand-ups or last-minute incredulous demands to write grammatically incorrect (yes, grammatically incorrect) colloquial copy for primetime news anchors—all directives from male news directors—she decided to exit the on-camera side of the business and instead produce the newscasts. Strong, decisive, take no bullshit … that's my wife. They say that men marry women who possess their mothers' traits. That's a fact.

Accordingly, I can only think I'm drawn to strong women because that's the way my mother was.

Now if you met my mom, you would never believe that she was a leader.

But she was.

Leaders lead in different ways. Sometimes they don't even realize they are leading, and sometimes their followers don't even realize they are being led. That's who my mother was. A quiet, decidedly fierce, determined, disciplined, loving leader of our small family. My older brother, dad, and I knew it. And we followed.

Despite her diminutive stature of 4-foot-11, maybe 100 pounds, my mom was a titan. Notwithstanding all of the frustration and the tremendous odds of daily survival stacked against her, odds that she faced quietly on a daily basis, she persevered. While continuing to be told figuratively or literally, in one way or another, that she and the family she guided, protected, and loved would not make it in America, my mom soldiered on.

Despite all that, she always found a way and never once complained.

The West End—Elm Motors

Little did we know that Mom would face a potentially existential challenge finding a safe way to just get out of the house to go to work one early morning at the end of July 1970. It was about 6:00 a.m. on a sunny, soon-to-be hot and humid day in New Bedford, Massachusetts, a relatively small working-class city fifty miles south of Boston, and the last big enclave you had to drive through to get to Cape Cod, when my mother, with a heightened sense of nerves, fear, and excitement rustled me awake. *Richie, Richie, wake up, wake up!*

She pointed out of our front room window and hurriedly showed me what seemed like an army of Massachusetts State Police that had amassed across the street in the abandoned remnants of the Elm Motors car lot, a Rambler car dealership that was burned out of existence the previous week by the Black Panther Party. The cops were preparing to do battle with members of the Black Panthers who had taken over our neighborhood a few weeks earlier. I rushed to the window that looked out on the car lot once filled with gleaming new cars. In the hazy early morning sun, I saw a phalanx of state police cars slowly streaming in a motorcade procession up the street in front of our tenement. The police cars parked on alternate street corners. Some pivoted and parked in the car lot. Others simply perched on the curb. Each car carried four Massachusetts State Police officers.

As each car stopped, the officers, all dressed in their majestic uniforms comprised of light-blue shirts, navy-blue striped pants, knee-high leather riding boots, and Canadian-Mountie–style, flat and stiff-billed lavender-colored hats, and aviator sunglasses, got out of their respective cars. They all had strapped X-shaped sheaths of ammunition belts across their chests bandolier-style, and stood impressively poised, in military-ready formation. One at each of the four corners of their respective police cars with what appeared to be shotguns firmly in hand.

They were ready to do battle.

The Boston chapter of the Black Panther Party seized the opportunity presented and quickly set up shop in Perichini's, the burned-out, white-owned convenience store. The proprietors of Perichini's had not only become fixtures in our community, but also ran the one store that kept many of us from starving, and that included many of the Black folks that burned the store down in a fit of Black Panther–fueled misplaced rage. You see, the Perichinis sold food to many of our parents on credit. They were our sole source of food, and the Black Panthers kicked them out and converted their storefront into an armed fortress. Plywood windows with gun turrets replaced the plate-glass window food displays.

With no money, kids like me would be sent to Perichini's to get food. After the Black Panther ambush, the store and the generous Perichini brothers were gone, forever.

The Perichinis had a handwritten, Black leather-covered lined paper ledger with various handwritten family names at the top of various pages that were separated by name—in alphabetical order. Some of the pages were stained with coffee, soda, or stuck together with the residue of the penny candies they handed out to kids like me who were not that thrilled about interrupted stickball games to do the going-to-the-store chore for Mom.

What as kids we didn't know and did not understand was that there was *no food* at home, and if we didn't go to the store, and if Perichini's didn't essentially give us the food items, we'd starve. As we eyed the many trays of penny candy inside the glass-covered countertops the vestiges of creeping age beginning to bend forward their respective spines, John Perichini or his brother in their Red Sox baseball hats would log our items, tally the total in the descending spaces beneath our family names, and our parents would pay what they could, when they could, if they could, which for many of us was rare. Each of us always received our choice of penny candy from Perichini's free of charge. My favorite was the red candy shaped like a nickel … we called it "red-cent." It was gelatin, chewy, and super sweet! Also, unfortunately for our family, the white-owned tavern that adjoined Perichini's store was also burned down by enraged Black folk following the senseless shooting deaths of our teenagers. Sadly, in New Bedford's West End, without Perichini's store, many Black families, including mine, would be without their consistent source of oftentimes free food. When this power struggle ended, the Black Panthers would return to their Boston hideouts, and the State Police returned to their suburban homes. Tragically, without Perichini's we had no food, and without the burned-down and demolished West End Tavern where my dad worked as a bartender, my father had no job.

Our sole source of money was my mom's brutal factory mill job at Aerovox. To fifteen-year-old me, the scene of ten state police cars, forty armed to the teeth with seemingly state-of-the-art shotgun weaponry, perched less than fifty yards from the window from which I spied them was breathtaking. To my mom, it was potentially the beginning of her worst nightmare—a massive shoot-out between the Black Panthers and law enforcement with bullets flying everywhere right in front of our home.

For a brief moment, she looked stunned.

But, in order to make me feel secure and safe, she exuded no fear. And, most importantly, she knew that no matter what, gunfight or not, she had to leave the relatively safe confines of our tenement and navigate her way safely to work. She risked getting fired if she missed a single day of work. Mom never missed a day. All of this was perpetrated by some young white renegades who harbored hate for Black folks and fired shots indiscriminately into a crowd of high school kids who congregated on the sidewalk of a summertime hangout spot about two blocks from our apartment. For more than two weeks following the senseless drive-by shooting death of a Black teenager, who was a friend of mine, our neighborhood quickly transformed into a cauldron of fire, bullets, marches, outrage and hate for anything and anybody white, no matter whom they happened to be. The combative faction of the Black community banded together to keep the neighborhood safe by keeping "whitey" out of our "hood," by any means necessary, and that included the police. The police were especially unwelcome because it already seemed like the white boys who had shot and killed one of our brothers, and seriously wounded three others would get away with murder. Despite an exact description of the car that carried the shooters, the license plate number and eyewitness accounts of the shooting, and distinct physical descriptions of the killers, no one was immediately apprehended. So, the Black folk decided to govern and police our West End neighborhood.

The West End was known as the more civilized of the various enclaves of Black folks in New Bedford. The South End was the bastion of unpredictable Black folks with a perceived penchant for violence.

In either the South End or the West End, if you didn't live in the projects, you were doing good.

We didn't live in the projects. The fact that my grandmother actually owned the tenement building in which we lived, we were considered to be "more better off" than most, a socioeconomic status that, combined with doing well in school, made me a target.

Notwithstanding the "more better off" economic categorization, we still consumed our share of USDA government food. Each Thursday, my after-school chores included grabbing the white Santa Claus–like laundry bag that my mom had prepared and dragging it to the laundromat.

When the wash cycle ended and after the wet clothes were stuffed into the dryer, I had to make the dreaded two-block journey to the government food post to retrieve our ration of free government edibles.

Everybody's favorite was the cheese. Government cheese was unquestionably the best cheese ever produced! The cheese was packaged in a rectangular eighteen-inch-long block covered by a cardboard covering. It truly was the best cheese ever. Apparently, by all accounts, it still is.

The second highest in demand of the limited, but consistent selection of the government delectable was the peanut butter. It too was incredible. The "PB" was ahead of its time.

Like all of the government canned goods, the peanut butter was presented in a small paint can-sized shiny silver container. In basic Black lettering, "Peanut Butter" was stenciled on the side of the can. When the container was opened, the unmistakable aroma of the peanut oil that floated on the top quickly wrapped around your nostrils. You had to mix the oil into the peanut butter. The texture was smooth, and the taste was gourmet. During the 1960s and early 1970s, peanut butter with the unmixed oil on top was considered cheap government peanut butter. However, in the 1980s peanut butter with unmixed oil on top actually became the gourmet peanut butter in the mainstream markets.

The government also famously provided white powdered milk, which was universally hated and was only consumed in the hardest of times, and green peas in a huge silver can. My mom hated both. Mixing that powdered milk with water was a surefire sign that your household had entered the depths of poverty, and we all knew it. In my house, it was a curse to be avoided at all costs.

Plus, the government never had any bags. So, you had to carry your government food through the streets for all to see you, and laugh at you because if you had government food, it was a sign that you were on welfare. And though we were all officially on welfare in some form or fashion, no one wanted to be on welfare—otherwise known as Aid for Dependent Children (ADC). "Ahhh, you all on ADC," was the unpleasant taunt you'd hear if someone spied you carrying that government food through the streets.

Walking through the streets with gleaming cans of government peas and peanut butter was a badge of temporary dishonor. My mom hated that I had to endure the brief periods of ridicule from similarly situated poor Black kids in our neighborhood. But she knew enduring the slights made me stronger. Again, notwithstanding our collective pride, the truth was we had to survive.

***

THE PANTHERS BURNED white-owned establishments in our hood. Debris from the fires was dragged out of the burned-out buildings to erect makeshift barricades comprised of burned furniture, desks, chairs, refrigerators, crumpled cars, and anything else portable, at the intersection of every street that leads into our neighborhood. Black citizens stood guard and only let Black folks pass into our community. Armed militia-like bands of rebels roamed and policed the streets. Shooting out streetlights during the day, and keeping white folks and police out at night. Each day, city crews attempted to replace shot-out streetlights. If they were successful, the Black militia would quickly shoot out the replaced bulbs. At night, the Black militia would roam our streets in search of white infiltrators. Occasionally, gunfire would erupt. I became adept at rolling out of bed and onto the floor at the first sound of bullets being fired.

My mom and I hung out together in our apartment. At that time, my dad was never home.

At about ten o'clock one night, while my mother and I were sitting in the kitchen, we heard police car sirens and speeding cars racing in the direction of our tenement. We instinctively glanced at one another, shut off the lights, and hit the floor just as we heard a car crash through the barricade on the street corner nearest to our front door.

Shots rang out.

We could hear the bullets hit the front door of our tenement as the abandoned, but still fast-moving car crashed through the wood fence that encircled the front and left side of the building and into what was our itty-bitty front yard. The driver fled to the safety of our ink-black dark neighborhood, a place the boundaries of which the police temporarily respected.

When the sun came up the next morning, we discovered three police-fired bullet holes in our front door.

In short, we were living in an armed enclave. It was us against them. But, despite the chaos, danger, and uncertainty, my mom got up each day and navigated the debris, spent bullet casings, and the humidity and went to work in a windowless, AC-less, red brick-walled, oven-like textile mill getting paid about a dollar per hour.

Her job was to place the tiny thin cardboard covering over the two-inch long, two-prong television tube, over and over and over again—for eight hours a day, five days per week, for forty years. She never complained, rarely missed a day of work, and proudly brought home her weekly paycheck, which after what are now characterized as FICA deductions, totaled about a paltry thirty-five dollars. My mom was tough.

Anybody enduring that daily grind had to be tough. Most of the workers at the Aerovox mill doing piecework, work considered to be inferior but necessary tasks relegated to the female workers—who were literally paid by the number of pieces—were tough, smart, and existentially reliable workers. You see, if the prong plug-ins on the back of television tubes manufactured by Aerovox were not properly covered with the cardboard cutouts, they were rejected and not able to be sold to the television manufacturers. Remarkably, if the female workers exceeded their weekly piece quotas, despite being paid less than the men, the women received small but welcomed bonus payments. My mom was a weekly recipient of the bonus monies. And we definitely needed the extra money. As an adult now, I can fully appreciate my mom's strength, wit, and resolve.

She silently figured out how to deal with and handle my dad, who was a brilliant, but markedly frustrated Black man in America. He was a light-skinned, handsome, athletic by-product of a white father (who he and we never knew), born and raised in North Carolina. He never had an opportunity to leverage his potential. As a teenager in the early 1940s, leveraging one's potential and intellect was not an option available to a young Black man in North Carolina, let alone anywhere in America.

As it happened for many Black men, World War II and the opportunity to pursue military service was their savior. My dad wanted to fly. So, he joined the Air Force only to be told that flight school was not an option for Black men, but chef school was a viable alternative. So, he became a chef and spent World War II as the chief mess hall chef on the island of Guam in the South Pacific. So, the Air Force gave him a profession. But, more importantly, World War II provided him with something better … he met my mom. Mom was a Wampanoag Indian and was also devoid of opportunity out of high school. So, she joined the military Women's Army Corps, affectionately known as the WACs. They met on the airbase in 1944 in Walla Walla, Washington, and married in 1945.

***

I DON'T KNOW if notions of equality circulated in my mom's mind when she joined the WACs, but I do know that she loved it. She told me so. She loved the discipline. She loved the camaraderie amongst the steadfastly strong women who performed whatever tasks they were assigned to assist the USA's war effort. She loved the sense of *team* and purpose.

Most of all, she says she loved the discipline of marching. Marching in sync, together as a unified unit of strong uniformed, military women, shoulder to shoulder in sharp formations with other strong women who had sacrificed to join the United States military, ready and equipped to serve their country. Strong, dedicated, disciplined, committed, tough, resourceful, unified women!! That's what my mom loved! That's who my mom was.

***

STRONG, AGGRESSIVE, INDEPENDENT quiet, determined. That was my mom and I really didn't realize it until she was gone. In fact, she faced her own death from lung cancer with strength and resolve and peace of mind. In her last weeks and hours on this earth, she was more worried about how my dad and my brother would deal with her death than she was about herself. Notably, she told me she wasn't worried about me. She said I was strong and would find a way to make it without her.

I wasn't so sure.

In a demonstration of her inner strength and awesome ability to just face reality and grab the bull by the horns as she always did in her life, in July 1997, my mom called me to essentially ask me for permission to die.

It was a Tuesday morning, and I was at my desk in the American Basketball League (ABL) offices in Palo Alto, California. My mom had been battling small cell terminal lung cancer for a few months. The doctors had given her six months to live after her March 1997 diagnosis. Ironically, I got the call just as I arrived at my hotel room in Cincinnati, Ohio to scout the NCAA Women's Basketball Championships.

Mom told me emphatically that she didn't want to do chemo. In her opinion, with only a 2 percent chance of defeating the cancer, what's the point? She told the doctors immediately when she was diagnosed that chemo was not an option. But I convinced her that despite the small chance that the chemo would save her life, it was worth a shot.

The doctors told us there would be three rounds of chemotherapy and they gave us the truth about the horrors of the treatment—weight loss, loss of hair, loss of appetite, loss of everything in an effort to save your life. That's the reality of chemotherapy. Poisonous chemicals are pumped into your bloodstream to kill the bad cancer cells and hopefully leave enough good cells alive to keep you alive when the chemotherapy ends.

It's a painful therapy. It was painful for my mom. Her inner strength allowed her to endure two rounds of this pain. As I look back on it, she did it for me because in truth, she really didn't want to do it. When she was done, she was done, and had to muster up the strength and courage to tell me. From the time as a skinny and diminutive grade-school boy, bullied and beat up in school because I was smart and favored by teachers who saw a bright future for me up to that point, my mom and I were together all the time. She was there as the anchor to get me through.

She was my protector.

And at ten o'clock that Tuesday morning in July, she called me. I answered the phone and I knew it was her. In a tired but soothing voice she said, "Richie, I want to ask a favor of you," and I said "What's that, Mom?"

She said, "Look I've made my peace with God and I'm ready to meet my maker, and the favor I'm going to ask of you, is that you let me do that, just let me go without going through this next round of chemotherapy. I've done a lot of things for you in your life, Richie, I'm just asking for this one favor, and I need you to agree with me because that's the only way that your dad and your brother will accept my decision."

At that moment I realized my mom's strength.

Facing certain death, she was calm, cool, and collected as she called and asked me for permission to die.

I gave her that permission.

And two weeks later, she was gone, but she left this world the way she lived it with quiet strength, peace, and on her own terms.

Clearly, my mother was a strong woman who was in control of her life to her last breath.

I guess in my mind I have always believed that like my mom, all women should have the opportunity to make the decisions that will control their existence.

All women should be offered the same equal opportunity to do just that.

And most particularly, all women in sports should be provided equal opportunities to play, and now, to get paid like their male counterparts in their respective professions. It's just that simple, but for some reason, the concept of equality for women is simplistically complex in our society.

I just never understood why women—the very being that gives us all life—and for that fact alone should be revered and profoundly worshipped—are not treated as equals.

And that is not a rhetorical question.

***

I CAN ONLY conclude that subliminally, my mother's life experience and my formative years living life absorbing her experience has directed me to work with independent, strong women who relentlessly and unforgivingly pursue their own paths in the face of huge institutional pushback.

The United States Women's National Soccer Team is one such group of independent, strong women, who have faced unrelenting, life-altering institutional pushback from the United States Soccer Federation. Despite their success, the USWNT has been treated like second-class citizens since at least 1999 in the wake of their first World Cup victory on American soil.

Make no mistake about it. The goal of the United States Soccer Federation is to promote men's soccer. The goal of the United States Soccer Federation is to promote the proliferation and growth of MLS, the men's professional soccer league. Ironically, the federation's ability to do just that—to promote the men's professional league—is truly dependent upon the revenue generated by the ultra-competitive, ultra-successful, United States Women's National Soccer Team.

Yep, that's right, the US Soccer Federation has leveraged the economic success of the women's national team over the past twenty years to bolster and benefit not only the men's national team, but MLS. Ironically the federation untruthfully, publicly proclaimed that the USWNT generated *less* revenue than the USMNT and that's why the USWNT did not deserve equal pay. Actually, as depicted in the US Soccer's financials, the exact opposite is true. In fiscal year 2014-15, US Soccer's financials disclosed that the USWNT accrued revenues of $20 million dollars and produced an operating profit of approximately $17 million dollars. Remarkably, the USMNT produced $5 million in revenues and an operating deficit of approximately $2 million. Simply put, the US Women's National Team produces more revenue than the Men's Team and is the *economic engine* of the United States Soccer Federation.

This writing is not the appropriate venue in which to explore the history of the development of MLS and the conflicting professional, personal, and financial relationships between and among executives and leaders of US Soccer and the executives, leaders and founders of MLS. That story is worthy of its own book.

But, with regard to this writing and the USWNT's quest for equal pay, suffice it to say that the principal goal of the United States Soccer Federation again is the growth of the men's professional game on the backs of the USWNT's on-the-field and concomitant off-the-field revenue-generating success for the US Soccer Federation.

So, when Hope Solo called me in December 2012 and asked me on behalf of the team for assistance in pursuing a better collective bargaining agreement and equal compensation from US Soccer, I was all in.

And that's my story. It's not complicated. It's not whimsical.

To me, the opportunity to take the US Women's National Soccer Team into the equal pay stratosphere was a natural challenge and the perfect next journey of my professional career.

2

American Basketball League (ABL) vs. NBA Commissioner David Stern

IN REMARKABLE PROGRESSION, in 1995, after almost twenty years of fighting for athletes in so-called amateur sports, I was presented the opportunity to pursue equitable compensation and equal opportunity for women in professional sports with the American Basketball League (ABL), the premier upstart women's professional basketball league and precursor to the WNBA.

I'm sure you've never heard of this league. Nobody dared or cared to talk about the origins of how the WNBA formed (especially under NBA commissioner David Stern's watch). More on that later.

A small group of visionary entrepreneurs in Palo Alto, California—all of whom were Stanford University alumni and rabid fans of Stanford's perennial NCAA champion women's basketball teams—decided in 1995 that it was totally unfair that after stellar college careers, our extremely talented female American college basketball players had to go overseas and risk their lives. Not only that, but they also recognized the financial reality that unfortunately, 28 years later still exists for WNBA players—as to why modern-day players like Brittney Griner was playing basketball in Russia, while her male counterparts could stay safe and sound in the USA and earn millions of dollars playing professionally in the NBA.

In fact, until the advent of the ABL, any and all attempts of creating a lucrative women's professional basketball league here in the United States failed—including the existing living failure, the WNBA.

Why?

Because not enough money is being paid to the female purveyors of the profession.

In the fall of 1995, Gary Cavalli, a former Stanford University sports information director; Anne Cribbs, a former Olympian; and Steve Hams, a technology expert at Hewlett-Packard, sat around the kitchen table and drew up a business plan that created the American Basketball League with the primary objective of providing talented, world-class, female college graduate basketball players an opportunity to earn a living wage playing basketball professionally in the United States of America.

So, in September 1995, in a low-lying bungalow-type modern office building on Embarcadero Road in Palo Alto, California, Hams quit his lucrative Silicon Valley job. Stanford alums Cavalli and Cribbs abandoned their successful public relations business, and without any financial resources and total uncertainty, totally committed to, created, and passionately launched the American Basketball League (ABL).

The commitment was real.

The goals were simple.

Create a women's professional basketball league, in the United States, that paid each player a minimum of $100,000 per year to play professional basketball *in-season* so that the nation's best would not have to leave home to pursue their profession. The ABL's obvious founding players would be the future Olympic Gold Medalists, the 1996 United States Women's National Basketball Team (USWNBT) ... a team that included icons Teresa Edwards, Rebecca Lobo, Jennifer Azzi, and Dawn Staley.

The ABL would pay each player $100,000 per year to stay home to play professional basketball, during the traditional basketball season.

Now that was not equal pay. That was not the same amount of money that the men in the NBA were being paid in 1995.

But it was enough money to convince the top women who played basketball in this country to stay in this country, to pursue their dreams and professions within the familiar confines of the United States of America.

Although not equal to the compensation enjoyed by the men who ironically dismantled their Players Association in 1995 to allow individual players to sue the NBA over compensation and the elimination of the "no strike no lockout" provision of their collective bargaining agreement, $100,000 was enough money to be considered fair and equitable, and enough money to constitute a livable wage that allowed them to pursue their profession at home.

More important than the money, these top female players—the best in the world at their craft— would not have to leave the safety of the United States to be a pro.

They would not have to literally risk their lives or loss of their liberty to be a pro.

They would not have to risk forfeiting their constitutional freedom as a United States citizen just to earn a living, doing what they do best, which was playing professional basketball.

Top college men didn't have to leave the US to pursue their profession to be able to earn a living wage to play basketball, so why should the women have to leave. Why can't they earn at least $100,000 a year playing professional basketball? That was the question in 1996, and unfortunately, for women playing professional basketball today in the WNBA, that question persists.

So, Cavalli, Cribbs, and Hams executed on their commitment, and the ABL was created.

So, what was my involvement with the ABL?

I was the vice president of corporate affairs and general counsel of the ABL and CEO Gary Cavalli was a good friend. I met Gary in 1977 when I was a graduate student at Stanford and trained with the Stanford track team. Since I was a sports lawyer and entrepreneur in the sports industry, Gary asked me to provide legal advice and counsel to the ABL.

By this time in my career, I had founded and for eight years owned and operated a sports marketing agency (Athlon Sports Management), owned and operated the City of San Francisco Marathon, created and operated a women's sports festival in San Francisco, had represented the 400-meter hurdler Edwin Moses and future NFL Hall of Fame wide receiver James Lofton, and had taught sports law for four years at my alma mater University of California, Hastings College of the Law, where I currently serve as a trustee of its foundation. Starting in late 1995, I provided my services pro bono to assist the development of the ABL's operational infrastructure, negotiated arena leases, and partnership deals with Reebok and Nike, finalized a twenty-four-game broadcast deal with ESPN, and created the ABL Standard Player Agreement.

It was exhilarating!

The ABL was a Silicon Valley, venture capital financed and structured, single-entity professional sports league. The ABL's founding players were the twelve on the USA National Women's Basketball Team that would go on to win the 1996 Olympic gold medal. Each player was an owner and possessed equity in the ABL, and the players participated in the operations and governance of the league. Notably, the ABL's first and ultimately largest investor was Joe Lacob, who went on to become the owner of the Golden State Warriors.

The NBA didn't pay much attention to the ABL while it was in its formative stages in 1995 and 1996. The founding players of the ABL—namely, the United States Women's National Basketball Team—were the "shoo-in" favorites to be gold medal recipients in the Atlanta 1996 Olympic Games.

The twelve players on that team were already worldwide stars. Teresa Edwards, Rebecca Lobo, Sheryl Swoopes, Lisa Leslie, Ruthie Bolton, Katrina McClain, Kate Smith, Dawn Staley, and the rest of the players, were all top names, the best female basketball players in the world. They all were United States citizens, but in order to earn a living playing their professional sport they each had to leave the US to do it.

Unfair.

Un-American.

So, on October 16, 1996, with the resolve and commitment to pay each player $100,000 per year, to have ten teams in ten different cities in the United States, playing professional basketball during basketball season, the ABL launched its inaugural season.

The commitment of Cavalli, Cribbs, and Hams was realized and the ambitious plan was executed when the first ball was tapped in the San Jose State basketball arena on that night in October, featuring the Atlanta Glory vs. the San Jose Lasers.

And the erstwhile general manager of the Lasers— in fact, the chief financier of the entire ABL—became the owner of the Golden State Warriors, none other than Joe Lacob.

Joe was totally committed to women's basketball. It took Gary Cavalli and me six separate negotiation sessions over tasty Italian dinners in San Jose, California, to convince Joe that our financial proformas made sense enough to invest an initial $3 million, to finance the start-up of the American Basketball League.

As I recount those sessions, given Joe's pristine level of financial sophistication in 1996, it's remarkable how relatively amateurish were the financial projections we presented Joe, who at that time was a humble, understated multimillionaire partner in the world's most successful venture capital firm Kleiner Perkins Caufield & Byers in Palo Alto. Joe earned his initial wealth in the medical biosciences industries and then became the head of Kleiner's Life Sciences Division.

So, our flimsy Excel spreadsheets with what now would appear to be sophomoric, proforma financial presentations were apparently revealing enough to convince this sophisticated investor to jump on board the ABL ship. Ultimately, Joe was so committed that, by year three of the ABL, he had invested upwards of $15 million *cash* in the ABL.

It was clear that Joe had a burning love for basketball, women's basketball in particular. He truly wanted to help propel the sport for women in the United States, and our plan of providing that opportunity for the top college players to stay home and play during basketball season and get paid a living wage doing it was compelling to him.

So, he wrote that first $3 million check in April 1996, and became the general manager of the San Jose Lasers five months before the inaugural ABL game.

Over the next three years, Joe demonstrated his undying total commitment to the ABL, to women's basketball, by calling us on the twentieth of each month. You see the league had ten teams, ten players each, and payroll was the biggest expense.

The ABL was the first and only pure single entity, professional sports league. Essentially, the league owned, operated, managed and financed all ten teams.

So, all revenues collected by ABL teams would flow directly to our central offices in Palo Alto, California. We managed the finances of the league. Our monthly "burn"—which is the term used in Silicon Valley for the amount of money it cost to operate a start-up company each month— was $1.5 million a month.

On or about the twentieth day of each month, we had a pretty good idea what our total ticket revenues collections would be at the end of the month. Incidentally, ticket revenue was our only source of revenue. Some months we'd have enough to cover the $1.5 million nut.

And some months we wouldn't.

In fact, most months we didn't have enough money. So, religiously, on the twentieth of each month, Lacob would call to ask us how much money we would need to cover our "burn" that month.

Some months the need would be $300,000.

Some months the need would be $500,000.

Some months the need would be zero dollars.

Some months it would be $1.5 million. We barely had enough revenue to cover our expenses. Ironically, with success—which we were having—our league operating costs actually increased.

Like a god, Lacob would literally come to our office and write us a check for whatever amount of money we needed to cover a burn rate that month. Some months the check would be $1.5 million. He'd write it.

Often, Lacob would roll up his sleeves and come to the office and literally work with us. He seemed to be in heaven learning the professional basketball business. It was as if he was earning his PhD in the professional basketball business as the lead financer for the ABL.

Lacob always displayed great humility and respect for all of us. He respected our commitment to the professional and personal financial risk we absorbed to take on this huge "game-changer" in professional sports.

Joe was and remains remarkably understated. He did not want or seek public recognition for what he was doing to make real the dream of a financially viable women's professional basketball league in the United States.

And in 1997 he made it clear that his ultimate goal was to own the Golden State Warriors. Yes, Joe Lacob told us that in 1997.

Thirteen years later in 2010 he made that his business reality when he bought the Warriors. But in 1997, Joe's goal and his objective was to create equitable earning opportunities for women to play professional basketball in the United States.

Equitable.

Equitable means fair. He wanted and we wanted a fair opportunity for top female basketball players, to earn a living pursuing their profession in the United States. And "equitable" meant getting paid a livable wage to play as professionals here in the US.

Now you would think that the powers that be—and the powers that be in professional basketball in 1995 was the NBA—would wrap their basketball-loving arms around these women and provide them an opportunity to earn a fair wage playing professional basketball at home. After all, the NBA financed USA Basketball, the governing body of the men's and women's national and Olympic teams. Accordingly, it only seemed natural that the NBA would step up and provide the best female basketball players in the world a professional opportunity.

Think again.

It was the absolute opposite. If the NBA and its Commissioner David Stern had their way, they'd crush the ABL before it even began to operate.

By 1995, Val Ackerman (ironically, today a member of the US Soccer Board of Directors) had served for ten years as senior counsel to the NBA and its Commissioner Stern. Ackerman will tell you now, what she told us in 1997. Absent the advent of the ABL, there would be no WNBA. Stern had absolutely zero interest in providing women and opportunity to play professional basketball and be paid an equitable wage. Ackerman told us that she had tried to convince Stern for at least a decade to create a WNBA.

Stern had *zero* interest.

Until the ABL came along.

Once the ABL was created and it became crystal clear in April 1996 that this upstart league would, in fact, launch its inaugural season in October 1996 sporting the 1996 US National Women's Basketball Team and soon-to-be 1996 Olympic champions as the 12 founding players of the ABL, Stern realized that the ABL was for real.

As a legitimate, professional basketball sports property, the ABL was going to compete for sponsors with the NBA—a sports product that at that time was not the most delectable of consumer brands, and was on the precipice of serious challenges with the players and their unhappiness with their compensation and other restrictions in their collective bargaining agreement. Additionally, the 1998-99 NBA lockout was looming and Stern was getting nervous.

At the time the NBA was flailing.

Soon, legal disputes with the Players Association would have the NBA flailing in a protracted 6-month player lockout, product uncertainty, and a post-lockout abbreviated 50-game, not-well received by the fans post-lockout season.

But since it was the only professional basketball game in town, and given network television's insatiable demand for "live sports," Stern had the best available "reality show"– a sports property that he could leverage into huge dollars for television sports.

Thus, the stage was set. The ABL, with Olympic-champion, female college graduates, playing fundamental, below-the-rim basketball was going to compete for a spot in the mind's eye of the basketball consumer. More importantly, the league could capture the hearts of women who make 80 percent of the consumer brand purchasing decisions, a fact and phenomenon that could lure NBA sponsors away from the sullied NBA brand and unintentionally occupy a big spot in what Stern considered his exclusive fiefdom of professional basketball. ABL sponsors could hurt the NBA's bottom line.

Between September 1995 and April 1996, David Stern watched the ABL as it developed and publicly announced cities, teams, venues, prospective sponsors, and of course lauded its twelve founding players—the United States Women's National Basketball Team—that later in the summer, would win the Olympic gold medal at the 1996 Summer Olympics in Atlanta.

Stern knew that we were negotiating sponsorship deals with Reebok and Nike, each of which would sponsor five of our ten teams.

He knew that we were negotiating with ESPN to have a twenty-four-game ABL schedule from October to April.

He knew we were for real.

He watched it.

But he never believed the ABL would happen. Why?

Because he knew that just as we had publicly announced, we needed the "Names, Images and Likeness" (NIL) of the twelve founding members for the ABL to have instant credibility as a new professional league. What most of the public didn't know, was that the NBA financially sponsored USA Basketball. USA Basketball is the national governing body for the United States Men's and Women's national basketball teams.

Importantly, USA Basketball also selected the twelve-member men's and women's Olympic teams.

The men's and women's 1996 US Olympic basketball teams would be selected on June 15, 1996. Needless to say, the NBA had huge influence with regard to who would be selected for the Olympic teams.

In April 1996, a couple of months before the US Olympic Women's Basketball Team would be named, the ABL was finalizing its deals with Reebok, Nike, and ESPN. We were so close to finalizing those deals that the time was right for us to send our historic inaugural ABL standard player agreements to all twelve founding members, all of whom happened to be the twelve members of the United States Women's National Basketball Team. Each player received, via fax, their first standard player agreements to sign to play with the ABL.

At the time the team was in their pre–Olympic team selection training camp in Colorado Springs. It was the final training camp before the June 1996 official selection of members of the Olympic team.

The Olympic basketball competition would be in September 1996. Since the ABL planned to launch its inaugural season and play its first game in October, the brand and marketing objective was to leverage an Olympic gold medal victory comprised of the ABL's founding players.

So, it was essential to have these players signed up to contracts before Reebok, Nike, and ESPN would finalize their deals with the ABL. If we didn't have these players' commitments in the form of signed standard player contracts, then Reebok and Nike and ESPN wouldn't believe that we really would be able to field a league.

We didn't anticipate any problems getting these contracts signed. Stanford star point guard Jennifer Azzi operated as de facto ABL/US team liaison. When we sent the contracts out, we expected to get faxed, signed agreements back immediately. We sent the agreements out to the players on April 16.

By April 17, there was no response. Five days rolled by. Not only did we not get any signed contracts from any members of the team, we had zero communication from anybody on the team.

Needless to say, we were worried.

Finally, six days had passed before Jennifer called us and told us that, when the NBA got word that the ABL had sent the players contracts, Stern flew three of his emissaries from New York to Colorado Springs to sit down with the team to discourage them from signing to play professional basketball with the ABL.

More importantly, it was clear to them, that anybody that committed and signed to play with the ABL might be risking their chance to be selected in June 1996 by NBA-sponsored USA Basketball's Olympic Team.

But Jennifer had called to tell us that seven of the twelve players were going to honor their commitments and sign the contracts to play in the ABL. Three other players were going to sign with what had not yet been announced would be the WNBA—Rebecca Lobo, Lisa Leslie, and Sheryl Swoopes—were going to be the first marquee players in that NBA-owned league.

Two other players, Ruthie Bolton and Katrina McClain, had opted to play in Turkey for more money than the ABL could pay.

Stern's first attempt to kill the ABL before it was officially born was to join forces with the NBA's major broadcast partner, NBC. In a hastily assembled impromptu chaotic press conference a couple of days after the ABL secured the seven signed contracts, NBC Sports president Dick Ebersol and Stern announced the advent of the WNBA. At that point, Stern and Ebersol could only tell the world that there would be eight WNBA teams in yet-to-be-identified major American cities, and that the WNBA would play in the summer starting in June 1997, right after the conclusion of the ABL's inaugural pro basketball season.

Unfortunately, that announcement chilled Reebok, Nike, and ESPN—existing NBA partners—from finalizing their deals with the ABL. Ultimately, only Reebok maintained their initial commitment to the ABL.

Reebok didn't know it at the time, but they were really our life-blood. We needed to be able to demonstrate to several investors that we had the corporate financial support ($5 million) from a major international shoe and apparel company. Absent that, we would've died in April 1996 months before the opening game.

And so, the battle for the throne of women's professional basketball in the USA began. We knew that Stern would pull out all stops to kill the ABL.

We also knew that the battle for sponsorship dollars had begun. We knew that if we didn't have a national over-the-air major network broadcast television deal within three years, there was no way we'd be able to survive. Without a deal on NBC, ABC, or CBS (on-air time that the ABL would have to purchase at a cost of several million dollars), we would have no outlet where sponsors could leverage and advertise their products, and without sponsors we could not afford a television deal. We had a real chicken-and-egg dilemma.

At the time there existed small, rag-tag, cable sports television networks. But all of the networks were regional. Except for ESPN, there were no national cable sports television networks.

So, we cobbled together a consortium of regional sports networks, the New England Sports Network (NESN), the Pacific Southwest Sports

Network (PSSN), The Pacific Northwest cable sports outlet (PNWN), and the Southwest Sports Network (SWSN), and put together a schedule of games that would be televised over cable television.

That "consortium" of regional cable sports networks was the ABL's TV deal!

And we were happy to have what we had.

Additionally, BET's Robert Johnson provided us a prime-time Saturday night slot for a game of the week broadcast. It was a huge rating success. Unfortunately, when Mr. Johnson announced his interest in purchasing an NBA team, we were informed that he received a call from the NBA *advising* him that any affiliation with the ABL would be detrimental to his dreams of ownership of an NBA Team. Consequently, after our second season with BET, they did not renew our relationship.

Our ratings were pretty good. Back then, if you had anything over a 1.0 cable rating, that was considered good. We were averaging 1 to 1.5 ratings for our ABL games. We played weekdays and weekends. Good cable ratings brightened our chances of getting an over-the-air, big television network deal, even if we had to purchase the television time.

Good cable ratings notwithstanding, Stern made it abundantly clear. He would do anything to make sure that we never got an over-the-air network broadcast deal with any of the big three networks— NBC, CBS, or ABC. Stern knew, and we publicly acknowledged that if after three seasons we did not secure a big-three broadcast network deal, we would die.

Collectively, Stern and the ABL were right.

That didn't mean we'd go down without a fight. The equality and equity objective for women in professional sports was real. We were going to do whatever was required to make it a reality. If that meant a back and forth with David Stern and the NBA, so be it.

Well, Stern felt the same way, and he was ready for blood.

We knew we needed sponsors to help finance the league. Absent sponsors, we needed investors who could provide the capital required to operate long enough to make an imprint in the sports world. In the business world, sponsors would convince everybody that playing women's professional basketball in the United States during basketball season was a valuable business opportunity.

Not all of the NBA owners were in David Stern's back pocket.

Chicago Bulls owner Jerry Reinsdorf characterized David Stern as a strongman. A strongman who wanted to own professional basketball, and anything that had anything to do with professional basketball, including televising professional basketball. Reinsdorf was the antidote to the *strength* of David Stern. Reinsdorf was a tough businessman in his own right. He was a seasoned, smooth but grizzly, take-no-prisoners tax lawyer and commercial real estate guru in Chicago. He made millions and millions of dollars in commercial real estate and knew his way around rough-and-tumble business.

Reinsdorf knew that the Chicago Bulls was a very valuable asset to the NBA. He also knew that locally, the Bulls was a very valuable cable television content asset. WGN was the local cable network. And in direct violation of the NBA Constitution that governs ownership of NBA franchises and the NBA's so-called "Superstation Rule" that limited the number of Bulls games he could license to be broadcast on WGN, the Chicago-based superstation cable television network, Reinsdorf sought to televise forty-one Bulls games instead of the twenty-five allowed by the NBA. So, Reinsdorf filed an antitrust lawsuit against the NBA in an attempt to stop the NBA from restricting the number of Bulls games televised by WGN. In 1996, the parties settled the dispute.

Remarkably, Reinsdorf was watching ABL games on what he called "the bird." The bird was satellite television, and it apparently allowed Reinsdorf to access some of the ABL televised games. He said he liked what he saw.

Reinsdorf liked the ABL's basketball product. He wanted to learn more about the ABL, and liked it so much that he called our offices and said he would like to have a sitdown with league executives to talk about investing.

So, I took a redeye flight from San Francisco to Chicago to be in his office the next morning, to pitch him on the ABL.

I was nervous. Being an owner that had enjoyed numerous NBA titles thanks to Michael Jordan, Reinsdorf was a very serious guy in my eyes.

When I got to his office, he said, *You have thirty minutes so start talking.* So, I gave Reinsdorf our thirty-minute investor-pitch. Everything you needed to know about the ABL—soup to nuts.

I concluded with, *Mr. Reinsdorf, this is why you should invest at least $3 million in the ABL and start an expansion team in Chicago.*

At the end of my presentation, he said he liked the product. He watched what he characterized as "the product" on the bird and he thought that the women were displaying fundamental, below the rim, honest basketball.

In a nutshell, he thought the ABL had a future. But, he cautioned that David Stern would do whatever is required to make sure that no one, absolutely no one infiltrates *his* professional basketball fiefdom.

"You see," continued Reinsdorf, "David thinks that he owns all of professional basketball and anybody who tries to encroach on anything that has anything to do with the business of professional basketball he will squash. That's what he tried to do with us when we signed WGN to televise the Bulls games locally, and that's what he's going to do to the ABL. He will do whatever is required to quash you too. Stern will kick you out of his professional basketball fiefdom."

Reinsdorf said that because he had just gotten out of a ten-year legal battle with Stern and the NBA over the WGN/Bulls cable television deal, he was not willing to take on another battle with Stern by investing in the ABL.

But he said, "I'll help you find an investor to establish an ABL team here in Chicago."

And he did.

Former Chicago Bulls player and three-point specialist Craig Hodges and his wife Allison stepped to the plate in late 1997 and invested $3 million to establish the Chicago Condors. We hired Jim Cleamons—former famed Chicago Bulls assistant coach for Michael Jordan's Chicago Bulls—to be the head coach of our Chicago Condors. The Condors would begin play in October 1998 in the University of Chicago's four-thousand-seat arena. Once the team and season were announced, the Chicago Condors games immediately sold out.

By the start of our third season in the fall of 1998, the ABL had proved that it could sustain. The WNBA started playing in the summer of 1997 to mixed reviews. People questioned whether anyone wanted to watch basketball in the summer. Others asked why are the women in the WNBA only being paid about $25,000 to play professional basketball when women in the ABL are being paid $100,000 to play?

These questions began to shine a negative light on David Stern and the NBA, which was financing the WNBA. It was clear that the NBA had zero financial commitment to the WNBA. The NBA was providing the finances that were required to just keep the WNBA alive. There was no appetite to actually promote professional women's basketball.

In 2023, the head of the Women's National Basketball Players Association (WNBPA): proclaimed that getting the right to have free access to priority lounges in commercial airports is a big economic benefit for the WNBA teams who are still flying commercial airlines and sitting in center seats to get to the games. Declaring that access to airport priority lounges free of charge is a huge benefit is shamefully indicative of the poor conditions and discriminatory economic environment in which the WNBA continues to exist and continues to exploit these great female basketball players.

Stern sent the word out to coaches of collegiate women's basketball teams that if they considered or decided to coach in the ABL, they would *never* get an opportunity to coach at USA Basketball training camps or for the US Olympic team. Coaching on the US national team and or the US Olympic team for women coaches was the leverage coaches needed to get better paying jobs in the collegiate ranks.

The word went out to ABL players that when the ABL folded, and only the WNBA existed, ABL players *would not get hired to play in the WNBA no matter how good they were.*

In 1997, in exchange for guaranteed salaries of $250,000 per year, "stardom" merchandising deals, and other financial rewards, the NBA began to recruit and entice top ABL players to renounce their commitment. Essentially, leave the ABL and come and play for the WNBA.

Notwithstanding those enticements and threats of future banishment from the WNBA, most of the ABL's original top players, and players signed after the 1997 and 1998 ABL and WNBA drafts (in which the ABL secured 95 percent of the top collegiate players in each draft) honored their *commitment* to the ABL, despite the constant pressure from the NBA.

And, to further the "in your face" operations of the ABL, in 1997, we hired two of the best women's basketball coaches in the world—Angela Beck of Nebraska and Old Dominion's Anne Donovan.

Our stature was elevating, but our finances were evaporating. Stern had put the proverbial squeeze on *any* NBA corporate sponsor that even thought about sponsoring the ABL. Spalding basketballs, State Farm insurance, and many others affiliated with the NBA would not even meet with us. ESPN would not even report ABL game scores on the air.

Television personality Robin Roberts loved the ABL and wanted to invest, but she was prohibited by ESPN, her employer at the time. She was successful in persuading ESPN to report the scores of our games after a heavy fan letter write-in campaign criticized the network for discrimination against female athletes and women's sports.

Every coach we recruited told us of the threats they received from the NBA if they considered and/or decided to coach in the ABL, and they said they couldn't risk their careers.

Players told us that they had been approached by the WNBA, but they were going to maintain the commitment to the ABL because the ABL was committed to them.

Notwithstanding, the late Nikki McCray, top ABL player from the University of Tennessee, was the first player that the NBA convinced with promises of fame and fortune to leave the ABL and play in the WNBA. The classic tactic of "divide and conquer" had now been deployed by the NBA to weaken the resolve and commitment of the ABL players to stick with the League that was committed to treating all of the players equally.

Twenty years later, US Soccer would utilize the same weapon of providing "economic benefits" of some kind for *selected* USWNT players –be it the benefit of keeping their jobs, meager incomes, and spots on the USWNT for players on the "bubble" and at risk of being cut, or access to lucrative endorsement deals with certain USSF sponsors for selected star players. The NBA and US Soccer deployed the same tactics to dismantle their respective players' commitment to equity (ABL) and equality (USWNT).

The next ABL player ravenously pursued by the NBA was Hall of Famer Dawn Staley.

Staley, currently the famed head coach of the University of South Carolina Gamecocks, was one of the ABL's inaugural players with the Philadelphia Rage. In fact, the Rage was originally based in Richmond, Virginia, as the Richmond Rage. It was Staley who lobbied us to move the Rage from Richmond to her hometown of Philly. Her star power would certainly be a fan draw in basketball-crazy Philadelphia.

So, we moved to Philly, and we played in the famed Palestra!

When we heard that the NBA was pursuing Dawn, Gary Cavalli and I flew from San Francisco to Philly to have dinner with Staley with the hope of trying to determine whether or not she would seriously consider an overture from the NBA to go to the WNBA. Well, later that same week, apparently, she got an offer from the WNBA that she could not refuse, and she left the ABL.

Losing Staley in 1998 before the start of our third and watershed "make it or die" year was the beginning of the unraveling.

Just as Sunil Gulati knew that in August 2016 if he fired Hope Solo, the greatest goalkeeper of all time an integral part of gold medal–winning US women's soccer teams between 2004 and 2012, he would send a message to the rest of the season team that if Hope Solo could be fired because of her commitment to equal pay, so could any of them.

David Stern knew the same thing about Dawn Staley. If Staley could be convinced to leave the ABL, that meant that the players could begin to believe that if they did not defect to the WNBA, they too could be left stuck on the ABL's sinking ship, and that their chances of survival would be slim to none.

However, the ABL did *not* lose any more players to the NBA. The remainder of the ABL players stayed the course. They courageously honored their *commitment* to the ABL.

Unfortunately, when Stern realized that the rest of the players would stick with the ABL, he made it his mission to scare away the only other option the ABL could access to survive—new investors.

Stern's mission was successful. On December 21, 1998, eight weeks into its third-season, the ABL shut down operations.

***

I FELT THE need to preface what you're about to read with the answers to the questions I've been asked with regard to why I think I'm qualified to tell the story about the quest of female athletes for equal pay in the world of soccer.

And again, as you can see with my ABL experience, it's because I lived it. I've been living it for at least thirty years. Let's just say I got a degree in female athletes' equity in sports during my stint with the ABL.

So, when literally out of the blue Hope Solo and the USWNT presented the opportunity to leverage my ABL equality for women in professional sports experience to lead the United States Women's National Soccer Team to the promised land of equal pay, I was more than qualified for the task.

As you'll see, what a daunting task it became.

3

History of Gender Inequality in the Workplace—Incremental Progress—A Snapshot

IT MIGHT COME as a surprise to many, but the Grand Slam tournaments in tennis awards prize money the same for men and women, yet that was not always the case. Thanks to Billie Jean King, the US Open was the first Grand Slam event to institute equal pay for men and women back in 1973. The other Grand Slams did not immediately follow suit until almost three decades later when the Australian Open became the second Grand Slam to implement equal pay in 2001. The French Open followed five years later. Wimbledon was the lone holdout, but finally caved and reluctantly granted equal pay only after Venus Williams penned an op-ed titled, "Wimbledon Has Sent Me a Message: I'm Only a Second-Class Champion" in 2006 for *The Times of London*.

"I'm disappointed not for myself but for all of my fellow women players who have struggled so hard to get here and who, just like the men, give their all on the courts of SW19. I'm disappointed for the great legends of the game, such as Billie Jean King, Martina Navratilova, and Chris Evert, who have never stopped fighting for equality. And disappointed that the home of tennis is sending a message to women across the world that we are inferior."

What this tells us is that these sorts of things don't happen overnight. The status quo of anything rarely changes in a short amount of time. More often than not these things can take years, or even decades as they did in professional tennis. Progress to equal pay, for whatever reason is, unfortunately, incremental. As exemplified by the USWNT's recent equal pay fight, it is usually the bloody two-steps forward, one-step backwards kind of progress.

That's why before we go deep into what transpired behind the curtains of the negotiating table of the USWNT's battle for equal pay, it is imperative to understand the history, trajectory, and the incremental 'victories" of women of disparate races, national origin, and societal status—naturally bound together by their gender battling the perennial powers that be for equality in the workplace.

Over the course of history, men have always been put on a pedestal when compared to women. Traditional gender roles had women taking care of children and doing chores in homes, while men were out working and earning money for the family. That was always the norm for centuries and did not change until the twentieth century.

It was not until World War II that more women entered the workforce, taking up work that was previously reserved for men who went out to war. Many women like my mother demonstrated their feelings of patriotism and equality by joining the US Armed Forces Women's Air Corps—the WACs—in full support of the WWII war effort.

This was the time when the famous Rosie the Riveter, the cultural icon, took America by storm. Between 1940 and 1945, the percentage of women in the workforce rose 10 percent from 27 percent to 37 percent. Nearly one out of every four married women worked outside their respective houses by 1945.

In June 1944, in what represented the first official act to elicit incremental change, New York congresswoman Winifred C. Stanley introduced the first equal pay for equal work bill, which made it illegal to pay women less than men for the same amount of work both in quality and quantity. Unfortunately, the bill was referred to the Committee on Labor, where it died and never got a chance to be seriously considered. Notwithstanding the defeat of the bill, the exercise was a valuable small step but huge beginning of what is still a tough incremental battle for equal pay.

Almost two decades later, President John F. Kennedy signed the Equal Pay Act (EPA) of 1963. The bill states that "no employer having employees subject to any provisions of this section shall discriminate, within any establishment in which such employees are employed, between employees on the basis of sex by paying wages to employees in such establishment at a rate less than the rate at which he pays wages to employees of the opposite sex in such establishment for equal work on jobs the performance of which requires equal skill, effort, and responsibility, and which are performed under similar working conditions." Essentially, the bill made it illegal for employers to pay their employees who were doing similar job duties differently based on their sex.

Needless to say, passage of the Equal Pay Act twenty years after Congresswoman Stanley's initial introduction of the bill in 1944 was the manifestation of the incremental work, education, and battles quietly fought in the intervening twenty years amongst Stanley's mostly white male congressional colleagues. Ultimately, this paved the way for the advancement of further equality rights for women in 1963. As will be revealed in this tome, after twenty-plus years of navigating the minefields and educating its young and older players alike about the realities of the macro discrimination in compensation they endured, the courage of the 2016 USWNT catapulted the push for equal pay to the red zone.

More importantly, the USWNT's true trailblazing activities have yielded substantial, tangible results. Indeed, the legacy of their epic battle has left a permanent blueprint and indelible path to equal pay that women in the general workforce can leverage in their respective workplaces.

Esther Peterson, the head of the Women's Bureau of the Department of Labor, and former First Lady Eleanor Roosevelt were prominent vocal supporters of the proposed bill, and the passing of the EPA was what really got the ball rolling for the equal pay movement.

However, like many bills or laws that are passed, initially, there were many categories of female employees that were excluded from the equal pay benefits. For one, the EPA did not cover occupations like executives, administrators, outside salespeople, and professionals. The Education Amendments of 1972 amended the EPA to include female workers previously excluded from the benefits of the EPA.

Incremental progress toward equality.

The Paycheck Fairness Act is a proposed bill that hopes to amend the EPA and was first introduced in 1997. The bill "punishes employers for retaliating against workers who share wage information, puts the justification burden on employers as to why someone is paid less, and allows workers to sue for punitive damages of wage discrimination." It also wanted to fund programs to help better train women to negotiate better wages. The bill has been introduced every two years since 1997—over twenty-five years ago—but still has not been enacted into law. One huge step forward in 1972, a stalled critical improvement, stymied twenty-six years in a row.

Incremental status quo.

The United Kingdom followed suit and enacted its own bill called the Equal Pay Act of 1970, which prohibited favorable treatment between men and women in regard to pay and work conditions of the workplace.

According to the Bureau of Labor Statistics, since the passing of the Equal Pay Act of 1963, women's salaries rose from 62.3 percent of men's earnings in 1979 to about 83 percent in 2023—which represents an incremental increase of 20.7 percent in average pay over a sixty-year period. That's a 3.45 percent incremental equalization of income per year for female workers.

Incremental progress.

Obviously, EPA was a huge positive for the women's movement, yet why is it that a bill which clearly stated that women should be getting paid the same as men for the exact same work still to this day has us even talking about pay disparity? Why can't women get paid the same money for doing the same job under the same work conditions as their male counterpart?

Over the decades we've learned about the revolutionary efforts of the Susan B. Anthonys or the Elizabeth Stantons who were prominent women's rights activists, but there have been countless other women who existed under the radar that you may not have heard about because they were not included in school textbooks.

However, these women waged and raged valiant fights for equal work, equal respect, and equal pay in their respective industries and professions. Remarkably, their individual efforts provided incremental elevation of the equal pay objective ... exemplified by their professional abilities to outperform their male counterparts.

Chien-Shiung Wu: The First Lady of Physics

The success of Christopher Nolan's blockbuster movie *Oppenheimer* highlighted the ascent of theoretical physicist Julius Robert Oppenheimer as he led the Manhattan Project during World War II and was responsible for the atomic bombs that dropped on Hiroshima and Nagasaki (the only use of nuclear weapons during an armed conflict in world history) in Japan. Yet the film failed to even mention the minorities and women who were responsible for the success of building the atomic bomb.

Chien-Shiung Wu was a Chinese-American female physicist who made significant contributions in the physics field, and was an integral part of the Manhattan Project during WWII. From the accounts of Wu's granddaughter, Wu affectionately called Oppenheimer "Oppie" and he called her "Jiejie (姐姐)," a term of endearment in Chinese meaning elder sister. Oppenheimer thought of Wu as knowing everything about the absorption cross-section of neutrons, a concept that would be utilized once she joined the Manhattan Project.

Dr. Wu was born in 1912 and grew up during the intersection of Chinese nationalism and the New Culture Movement, which openly questioned traditional Confucian values. Both her parents valued education for both genders, as her mother was a teacher, and her father was an engineer. Her father openly advocated for women's rights as he opened a school for girls after Wu was born.

After getting accepted to the University of Michigan, she boarded the SS *President Hoover* in 1936 and was set on advancing her career in physics. With the arrival of communist rule in 1949, it would be the last time she would see her parents because of how impossible it would be to go back and forth.

Although she was accepted to the University of Michigan, Dr. Wu decided to attend the University of California, Berkeley after visiting the campus and meeting her future husband, physicist Luke Chia-Liu Yuan and seeing the Radiation Laboratory, whose director Ernest O. Lawrence would go on to win the Nobel Prize for Physics in 1939. It also did not help Michigan's case of luring Wu after she learned that women at the university were not allowed to use the front entrance.

"In China there are many, many women in physics," Dr. Wu once said. "There is a misconception in America that women scientists are all dowdy spinsters. This is the fault of men. In Chinese society, a woman is valued for what she is, and men encourage her to accomplishments, yet she remains eternally feminine."

After Berkeley, Dr. Wu and her husband moved to the East Coast, where she initially joined Smith College as an assistant professor but later joined Princeton University as a faculty member, becoming the first woman staff member in their physics department.

In 1944, Wu was recruited to the Manhattan Project laboratories at Columbia University to work on the process of uranium enrichment, which was the process of separating uranium into two types of isotopes by gaseous diffusion. Her findings in uranium helped fuel the atomic bombs that were being developed in a Tennessee facility.

Due to the aftermath of what the atomic bombs did in Japan, Wu later distanced herself from the Manhattan Project and told Taiwanese President Chiang Kai-shek in 1962 to never build nuclear weapons.

Wu spent the rest of her career working at Columbia University. One of the most important contributions she made to physics was a series of experiments where she tested the concept of the "conservation of parity." This essentially meant that there was a rudimentary symmetry in the behavior of everything in nature, including atoms. In ultra-cold temperatures, Wu observed beta decay in experiments that tested parity laws.

The theory went on to win a Nobel Prize in 1957, however, Wu was not given any credit, and instead all the recognition was attributed to her male colleagues (who were also Chinese). They had come up with the theory, while she was the one who actually tested it. It is widely considered to be the biggest snub in Nobel Prize history.

"Although I did not do research just for the [Nobel] prize, it still hurts me a lot that my work was overlooked for certain reasons," Dr. Wu wrote to another physicist, Jack Steinberger, later on.

She campaigned for gender equality throughout her profession and even corrected anyone who called her by her husband's surname. She was also insistent on being paid equally as her male colleagues at Columbia.

I wonder whether the tiny atoms and nuclei, or the mathematical symbols, or the DNA molecules have any preference for either masculine or feminine treatment, Dr. Wu said in 1954 at a MIT symposium speaking out against gender discrimination.

Even though she was unable to gain any recognition with the Nobel Prize, Dr. Wu was able to attain much acknowledgment in other regards. She was elected to the National Academy of Sciences in 1958, making her only the seventh woman at the time to achieve this. In 1975, she was the first woman president of the American Physical Society. Additionally, she was the first woman to win the Comstock Prize in Physics given by the National Academy of Sciences. In 1978, she was the inaugural person to receive the Wolf Prize in Physics.

Dr. Wu succumbed to the complications of a stroke in 1997 in New York City. Her granddaughter, Jada Wu Hanjie, once recalled, "I was young when I saw my grandmother, but her modesty, rigorousness, and beauty were rooted in my mind. My grandmother had emphasized much enthusiasm for national scientific development and education, which I really admire."

Dr. Wu's steadfast resolve to be recognized as an intellectual equal by her male colleagues, and more importantly paving the way to equal pay on the faculty of Columbia University was, again, incremental but vital to the cause of equality in academia.

Addie L. Wyatt

Reverend Addie L. Wyatt was one of the earliest known female civil rights activists and a union leader. She was the first African American woman elected as a vice president of a major labor union (Amalgamated Meat Cutters Union) in 1953.

Born in Brookhaven, Mississippi, in 1924, Wyatt was the oldest daughter of eight children. She grew up during the Great Migration and like many southern Black families, left their Jim Crow regions and moved to unfamiliar places for better opportunity and treatment. When Addie was four years old, two Black men were lynched by a mob in the vicinity of the Wyatt household. Two years later, her father got into a fight with his boss who was white, and abruptly left town. The rest of the family soon followed him to Chicago. In addition to the discrimination they dealt with in the South, the Great Depression happened as Wyatt was going through her childhood, and impacted her family profoundly. So, at the age of six, her family moved to Chicago hoping to seek better employment opportunities and avoid the mistreatment of Blacks.

"When we were small in the South, I knew that Blacks were discriminated against," Wyatt once said about first discovering racism and discrimination. "At that time, we were called "colored" and colored people were discriminated against. It wasn't until I started in the paid workforce of this nation that I discovered that women were also discriminated against. Facing the discrimination as a race and as a woman, something woke up within me. I remember my mother said life can be better—you have to help make it so. I would raise the question in my mind. What can I do? I have got to do something. I can't tolerate, I can't deal with racism and sexism."

When she was sixteen years old, she married a postal finance clerk and had two sons. Because her father was marred with an illness and her mother died at the young age of thirty-eight, Wyatt had to care for some of her younger siblings. With responsibilities mounting, she tried to get a job as a butcher for the Armour and Company. She was immediately kicked off the work line, but as she left, she saw a group of white women in line applying for clerical jobs. She managed to get in the line and take a typing test, which she passed with flying colors. She got the job as a typist for the Armour and Company in 1941. However, on her first day of work, she was redirected to the factory floor and joined the other African American women to pack stew in cans for the military.

"I was so disappointed and I began to inquire among the others there about the job and say to them that I was just there temporarily because I'm going to work in the office as a typist," Wyatt said in 2002. "They just snickered because they knew what I didn't know at that time. But as I worked there and began to inquire about salary, I was told that the salary was sixty-two cents an hour for women. Of course, at that time if you were a typist, you might have earned something like nineteen dollars a week. If you were Black and light–complexioned, you might have earned something like twelve dollars a week. And if you were Black like me and got hired at all, you might have earned something like eight dollars a week. Of course, twenty-four a week was more money than I had ever seen in my life and I decided to stay there on the line packing stew in a can."

In a study done by the National Women's Law Center in 2019, a Black woman typically expected to lose $946,120 over her career compared to that of a man, and would need to work twenty-six years more just to make up that deficit.

After that experience on her first day of work, Wyatt was determined to fight for what she thought was equality. Wyatt realized that unions did not discriminate against the workers, and joined the United Packinghouse Workers of America. By 1955, Wyatt was working for the union full-time, which looked over workers in a five-state region. She was moving up the ranks fast within the union and after becoming vice president in 1953, she soon was elected president for the UPWA Local 56 in Chicago.

The UPWA got intertwined with the Civil Rights movement, thanks in large part to Wyatt. In 1956, her union was the first one to invite Dr. Martin Luther King Jr. to visit Chicago to present him with funds for the Montgomery Improvement Association. She and her husband, Claude, formed a close bond and working relationship with Dr. King and were arrested with King in Selma, Alabama.

She applied the union's antiracist and antidiscrimination laws to fight against race and gender-based discrimination in the workplace. Her union was able to achieve union contracts with "equal pay for equal work" conditions for white, Black, and Hispanic workers well before the EPA went into effect in 1963.

In 1962, Wyatt's work caught the eye of former First Lady Eleanor Roosevelt, who led the US Commission on the Status of Women. President John F. Kennedy appointed Wyatt to the Committee of Labor Legislation's panel. Her work was the blueprint that eventually became the Equal Pay Act of 1963.

"Racism and sexism is an economic issue," she once said. "It was very profitable to discriminate against women and against people of color. I began to understand that change could come but you could not do it alone. You had to unite with others. That was one of the reasons I became a part of the union. It was a sort of family that would help in the struggle."

Wyatt spent the 1970s focused on lifting minorities through the work with her union. In 1972, she helped form the Coalition of Black Trade Unionists, which enlightened Black labor workers to "share in the power of the labor movement at every level." Two years later, she formed the Coalition of Labor Union Women, which essentially gave women a voice in the fight for labor rights.

All this work garnered her national attention and in 1975, *TIME* chose her as one of its Women of the Year alongside Billie Jean King, First Lady Betty Ford, and the first elected Black congresswoman, Barbara Jordan. Wyatt was recognized by *TIME* for "speaking out effectively against sexual and racial discrimination in hiring, promotion, and pay."

In 1979, Wyatt became the first African American woman in a high-level executive position at an international union, when she became the vice president of the United Food and Commercial Workers.

Besides her work as an activist and with the union, she became an ordained minister in 1955. Along with her husband, she founded the Vernon Park Church in Chicago. Wyatt officially retired from working full-time with unions and instead focused on her ministry. The couple's ministry spanned forty-four years and included operating two churches, with the second one that included one thousand seats.

Wyatt was influential, especially in the Chicago community. Lonna Saunders, a Chicago attorney, said that she was a mentor to President Barack Obama when he was still finding his way as a young man. In

2012, Obama called her a "champion of equality and a fierce advocate for working Americans" in a letter read at Wyatt's funeral.

"I had been a leader in the organized labor movement, but our women's movement started in the organized labor movement. Because one of our greatest themes was to make life better for women," Wyatt explained about why she got involved in unions. "They told me it was because women didn't deserve to earn as much as men, and that women did not work as hard as men and they did not have to do heavy work like mine. Any more of that turned me on. It really turned me on. Because I guess one of the reasons it turned me on was because so many women felt that way too not just me.

"We had to educate ourselves. We had to stir them up and we had to talk to our women about why we were really discriminated against. It has nothing to do with who has to do the more difficult jobs. It was because we were female and it was profitable to discriminate against somebody, and the somebodies that were discriminated against were those who were of color and those who were female; also, those who lived in geographical locations that were in the South. We had to make a change."

Lilly Ledbetter

Lilly Ledbetter is someone whose name will forever be etched with the equal pay movement. Born in Jacksonville, Alabama, in 1938, Ledbetter became a national activist for equal pay.

In 1979, she took a job as an overnight supervisor at the Goodyear Tire and Rubber Company plant in Gasden, Alabama. She would spend the next nineteen years working for Goodyear until she retired.

Ledbetter and Goodyear had a signed contract that she was not allowed to discuss salaries. Yet, she received an anonymous note just before her retirement that listed the salaries of fifteen men who performed the same duties as her. She realized that by the time she was retiring, she was earning $3,727 per month compared to the fifteen men, whose salaries ranged from $4,286 to $5,236 per month.

"Reading the scribbled words, my heart jerked as if hit by a lightning bolt," Ledbetter recalled in an article for *Huffington Post*. "The note showed my salary, listed next to the three male managers' salaries: I was earning $44,724 while the highest-paid man earned $59,028 and the other two followed close behind, earning $58,464 and $58,226. Maybe I was seeing things. Maybe this note was a serious mistake or a bad joke, though I knew in my gut it wasn't."

Goodyear determined annual salary increases based on each individual's performance reviews conducted by employees' supervisors at the conclusion of each year. Each employee's performance was ranked compared to other salaries for employees performing the same tasks and then supervisors would recommend a salary increase based on the company's salary guidelines.

Despite Ledbetter receiving a Top Performance Award from Goodyear, her supervisor had ranked her "at or near the bottom" compared with other area managers in almost every year between 1992 and 1997. By 1997, her salary was 15 percent lower than the lowest-paid male area manager and 40 percent lower than the highest-paid area manager.

In 1998, her supervisor again ranked her performance as on the bottom tier of area managers and denied her a raise. By January 1998, she was reassigned to work as a manual laborer technology engineer even though she was in her sixties.

"As I deliberated about what to do next, I felt shame and haunting humiliation deep in my bones," Ledbetter wrote in the *Huffington Post*. She noted that the obvious disparity in her compensation when compared to what her male counterparts were paid to do the same work indicated that she was born the wrong sex. Notwithstanding being two years from retirement and possibly losing her pension, Ledbetter knew she had to take the risk and stand up for what is right. She knew she had no other choice. Ledbetter also acknowledged that it would be the hardest fight of her life with no guarantee of success.

In March of that year, not being able to afford a lawyer, Ledbetter filed a questionnaire under Title VII of the Civil Rights Act of 1964 with the Equal Employment Opportunity Commission (EEOC). In July, Ledbetter officially filed a formal charge of discrimination that "she had received a discriminatorily low salary as an Area Manager because of her sex." These set off a statutory time limit that restricted future litigation under Title VII to incidents that occurred within 180 days prior to the date she filed her questionnaire.

In November 1999, Ledbetter filed a lawsuit against Goodyear in the United States District Court for the Northern District of Alabama, alleging that their salary protocols were unlawful and consequently led to unfairly low paychecks. Ledbetter testified that at the start of her career, she earned the same salary as her male colleagues, but at the time of her retirement in 1998, she was paid 40 percent less than those same employees.

In 2003, the jury ruled in her favor that Goodyear had sullied Title VII and that it was likely that Ledbetter was paid a lower salary based on her sex. She was awarded $3.8 million in the process.

However, Goodyear appealed the judgment, arguing that the Title VII statutory period restricted Ledbetter's equal pay claim to within 180 days of the date she initially filed the questionnaire. Essentially, Goodyear contended that her claim be restricted only to her performance review in 1997 and her supervisor's rejection of a raise in 1998. The Eleventh Circuit deemed the appeal successful and made its way all the way to the Supreme Court.

In a 5–4 motion, the Supreme Court ruled against Ledbetter, stating that "she could have, and should have, sued" when the pay decisions were made, instead of going beyond the 180-day statutory period. Since her claim was filed outside the 180-day window, she was not awarded any monetary amount.

"We sought justice because equal pay for equal work is an American value," Ledbetter said after the ruling. "That fight took me ten years. It took me all the way to the Supreme Court. And, in a 5–4 decision, they stood on the side of those who shortchanged my pay, my overtime, and my retirement just because I am a woman."

In an unusual event in SCOTUS rulings, Justice Ruth Bader Ginsburg disagreed with the majority and read a passionate dissent. Over the next ten minutes, she argued that pay discrimination is much different from other forms of discrimination because it occurs in "small increments" and only becomes evident over time. According to recent studies, women still make about 82 cents for every dollar that men earn.

Ginsburg wrote in her dissent, "Our precedent suggests, and lower courts have overwhelmingly held, that the unlawful practice is the current payment of salaries infected by gender-based (or race-based) discrimination—a practice that occurs whenever a paycheck delivers less to a woman than to a similarly situated man."

Inspired by what Ginsburg had said, some Democratic members of Congress drafted and introduced the Lilly Ledbetter Fair Pay Act, which essentially threw out the 180-day statute of limitations for pay discrimination in 2007, the same year of the SCOTUS ruling of the Ledbetter case.

Congress passed the bill, but it died in a Republican majority Senate. Republicans accused Democrats of trying to score political points ahead of the 2008 presidential campaign.

However, the bill was reintroduced in January 2009. This time, it passed through the Senate on a 72–23 vote, and the Lilly Ledbetter Fair Pay Act was signed on January 29, 2009, just nine days after President Barack Obama took office, and the first bill that he signed as president.

The law effectively would amend Title VII of the Civil Rights Act of 1964, and the 180-day statute of limitations would reset with each new paycheck that was affected by that singular discriminatory action. Quite frankly, the law allowed women to contest pay irregularities from any period of their careers.

Today, Ledbetter continues to fight for women's equal pay in the workforce. She wrote her own autobiography titled *Grace and Grit: How I Won My Fight for Fairness at Goodyear and Beyond* in 2012, and her life is being portrayed in a film where Oscar-nominated Patricia Clarkson will be playing Ledbetter.

Achieving something as simple as equality takes time and patience. Stanley first introduced an equal pay bill in 1944, and even today we're still talking about women earning eighty-two cents to the dollar for their male counterparts. Look at the Paycheck Fairness Act that is still ongoing. It has been introduced a whooping thirteen times over the past two decades and yet, is still trying to get passed because of the persistence and patience of women's rights advocates.

Like the circumstance with Ledbetter's case and the 180-day statute of limitations, even the bills that are passed have certain conditions written within the fine print that scream anything but equality. In her fiery Ledbetter dissent, Justice Ginsberg aptly noted that pay discrimination is different than other forms of discrimination because it occurs in small increments over time. It's not until the incremental accrual becomes so egregious that its ugly countenance is revealed to the world —and the horrifying disparities in pay must be addressed.

Decades of oppression and pay discrimination was meted out by the USSF against its most prized possession—the USWNT. Despite being the best in the world for almost thirty years, the incremental wage gap between the USMNT and the USWNT accumulated to the point where in 2015, the USWNT were earning 75 percent *less* than their male counterparts doing the exact same job, under the same work conditions.

And yet, notwithstanding the horrible realities, despite the USWNT's courageous, relentless battle for equal pay, the powers that be at the USSF continue to deny the USWNT equal pay.

Indeed, as aptly noted by Ms. Wyatt, it was and remains profitable to discriminate against females. With regard to the sport of soccer, it can be said that because the USWNT is comprised of females, it's profitable to discriminate against them by paying the women in the sport less than the men. Simply stated, because US Soccer's cost of producing its most valuable asset—the USWNT—upon whose success the federation leverages, sells, and collects hundreds of millions of dollars in television and corporate sponsorship rights fees—is at least, from a USWNT player compensation comparison, 75 percent less than the player compensation expense of the USMNT product, the USWNT is by US Soccer's admission the economic engine of the federation.

In fact, the federation's economic incentive to keep the compensation paid USWNT players at low levels thereby increasing the profit margin is so strong that the federation has used intimidation, veiled threats of economic harm and loss of jobs and careers against the USWNT to encourage and some might say extort the players to resist the urge to fight for equal pay and better working conditions.

Faced with the looming threat of retaliation in the form of loss of income, jobs and their professional soccer careers, Hope Solo engaged Jim Trusty, former chief of the Department of Justice (DOJ) Organized Crime Division and an expert in RICO—who, incidentally signed off on an approved all civil and criminal RICO cases pursued by the DOJ, including the DOJ's RICO prosecution of FIFA executives, and most recently counsel for President Donald J. Trump in the classified documents case—to investigate and, if sustainable, pursue a civil RICO action against the US Soccer Federation.

In a prospective civil RICO case against US Soccer, the USSF, Soccer United Marketing (SUM), and MLS would be the purported "racketeering enterprise" defendants, while the federation's use of intimidation and threats of lost jobs and careers against the USWNT players for pursing equal pay would be the requisite "predicate act" required to substantiate and sustain a civil RICO claim against US Soccer.

4

From Conciliation to Confrontation: The Player Power Syndicate and the Genesis of "The Cycle"

DECEMBER 2012 MARKED about fourteen years since John Langel began his representation of the United States Women's National Soccer Team. Officially, Langel was the executive director and general counsel of the US Women's National Team Players Association (USWNTPA), which is the USWNT players union and the team's official National Labor Relations Act collective bargaining unit.

I never really asked the team much about Langel or his representation of them.

For that matter, I never had the occasion to ask Langel about his tenure working with the team. Somehow, his departure and my assumption of his role all seemed a bit awkward. But, by all accounts, Langel had served the team well.

And in life, all things run their course.

Notably, it was also clear that many if not all of the players saw Langel as a kind of father figure to the USWNT. They cared about him. He cared about them. After all, he started to represent them officially in late 1998 about one year before the USWNT's remarkable second World Cup championship, and the likewise incredible and unexpected onset of disrespect and abuse of the team perpetrated, remarkably, by none other than the US Soccer Federation.

At that time, projecting ahead and contemplating all of the new-found fame and opportunities the players thought winning the 1999 World Cup might bring, the players knew they needed representation. Though I don't think they were quite sure as to why they needed a lawyer.

But, before long, it became clear that instead of the World Cup victory being viewed by US Soccer as a tremendous opportunity to market and promote its most valuable asset — the USWNT—conversely, US Soccer regarded the success of the team as a burden. Furthermore, USWNT was seen as a direct threat to what the federation regarded as the primary objective of the federation, which was and remains the growth and development of the United States Men's National Soccer Team and its professional, unofficial affiliate, Major League Soccer (MLS).

According to Caitlin Murray's book entitled *The National Team*, the federation's apparent, yet unimaginable disdain for the World Cup–champion USWNT became more than clear with the federation's actions, or lack thereof, during the months and entire year after their 1999 World Cup victory.

To begin, after their monumental triumph that thrust the team into national and worldwide prominence, instead of scheduling more games (friendlies) to showcase the USWNT World Cup champions in the USA, the USSF scheduled *fewer* USWNT games and booked the team on a tour in Africa.

Instead of selling the USWNT to corporate sponsors, the federation redirected companies eyeing US Soccer sponsorships to the men's team.

Instead of engaging a robust public relations plan to promote the USWNT, the federation strangely proclaimed the two years after the World Cup victory as the USWNT "dark years" during which fewer games would be scheduled, and minimal if any dollars would be spent marketing the team. Notably, scheduling fewer games for the USWNT meant fewer tickets would be sold to USWNT games, thereby generating less revenue for the USWNT. This fact would become the USSF's legal justification for paying the USWNT less than the USMNT—the women generate less revenue than the men, so we pay them less.

As chronicled in *The National Team*, in 1998 before the 1999 World Cup, Mia Hamm and Langel recognized the federation's lack of respect and interest in the USWNT and sensed the team was on the brink of greatness. Thus they hatched the idea of creating a post–World Cup and or Olympic championship "Victory Tour" during which the USWNT would travel to five indoor soccer venues in major American cities and play exhibition games.

Remarkably, without any USSF involvement, Langel and Hamm secured a $1.2 million sponsor and executed the first five-game Victory Tour after the 1999 World Cup victory. Each of the twenty-four players received $60,000 to participate in it.

Unbelievably, US Soccer contemplated stopping the lucrative tour by threatening to seek an injunction in federal court claiming in part that the team misappropriated US Soccer's logos and other intellectual property by planning to conduct the tour and securing sponsorships in which sponsors would have illegally exploited US Soccer's assets—one of which is the USWNT—without the USSF's authorization.

Clearly, Langel understood the challenges the team faced, and with his partnership with Hamm and the advent of the Victory Tour, he clearly embraced the team's value. But US Soccer are the masters of determining how to turn the tables on the team to ultimately weaponize anything good that evolved from the team's initiative and to use it against the team.

Langel and the Victory Tour were no exceptions.

In 2000, the USSF bought the Victory Tour from the players in exchange for $2.2 million, and over the next ten years increased the games from five to ten. Player income rose from $60,000 to $75,000 to participate and the federation "weaponized" the tour by imposing an "all or nothing" metric on the players. To get the entire $75,000, each player had to play all ten games. The Victory Tour games were huge revenue generators for the US Soccer Federation, and ten additional, poorly compensated workdays for the team. If a player missed any one of the Victory Tour games, they did not get paid at all. If a player appeared in all ten games, she would receive $7,500 per game. If they played nine games but missed the tenth, they did not get paid at all.

Unfortunately, the federation's purchase of the Langel-Hamm "leverage"–creating Victory Tour, and the advent of a Langel-USSF transactional relationship, apparently combined to facilitate the trans-formation of Langel's initial rebel, hard-nosed anti–US Soccer repre-sentation of the team in 2000, to that of a seemingly softer, conciliatory posture toward US Soccer by 2012.

The USWNT sensed the change.

No Leverage in 2000, 2004, and 2008

By all accounts, Langel had great instincts. He understood that the team was woefully underpaid and totally disrespected by the federation. Furthermore, he initially seemed to be determined to get them paid and appreciated. Langel was well liked and respected by the players, and up until 2012, they all believed that he had zealously represented their interests when negotiating the team's 2004, 2008, and 2012 collective-bargaining agreements with US Soccer. But, incredibly, up until 2012, the highest amount of money that the top players had earned per year was $70,000.

Additionally, there were three tiers of compensation — Tier 1 for the top players, Tier 2 for the middle-of-the-road players, and Tier 3 for everyone else. Which tier certain players occupied was determined subjectively by the head coach.

***

TO BE CLEAR, before Hope Solo called me in December 2012, I didn't really know anything about the USWNT. In fact, I didn't know much about soccer. Growing up, I had exposure to the game. My hometown of New Bedford, Massachusetts was affectionately referred to as "Little Lisbon" due to its large Portuguese population to whom soccer was the sport of choice.

Notably, in my junior year of high school, we won the state and New England soccer championships. Our top player was goalkeeper Eddie Rodrigues. In our yearbook there is a photo of Eddie looking quite bored, leaning up against the goal he defended during a game. Our defense was so good that rarely did opposing teams penetrate the zone in front of the goal to provide him any action.

In fact, as exemplified by Eddie's posture in the yearbook picture, I thought soccer was the most boring endeavor in competitive sports. You have twenty players running up and down an oversized football field for ninety minutes with no timeouts, usually little to no scoring, and then often the winner is decided by shooting penalty kicks into essentially an open net?

Really?

That was my warped perspective about the game of soccer.

I had zero interest in the sport.

Accordingly, I did not know anything about how much the players on the men's or women's team were paid. I surmised that given the USWNT's thirteen years of flawless play, they must be earning a couple of hundred thousand dollars per year.

Needless to say, I was shocked to learn that the top Hall of Fame–bound champions of the sport Abby Wambach, Christie Rampone, Hope Solo, Alex Morgan, Carli Lloyd, and others occupying the top tier of compensation were only being paid $70,000 a year!

Shocking.

More shocking, the players on Tiers 2 and 3 were earning less, $50,000 and $30,000 respectively.

And these were collectively bargained earnings!

To add insult to injury, US Soccer treated the players like second-class citizens. The team traveled on low-cost Southwest Airlines, sat in center seats, stayed in three-star Holiday Inns, rented panel vans for transportation, practiced and played games on life-threatening artificial turf, received paltry per diem, endured 250-day per year in-residence training camps, had no maternity leave, no 401(k), no vacation time, minimal health insurance, and played thirty-plus games per year for $70,000, $50,000, and $30,000 per year?

Clearly, sans complaint, the world champs endured decades of shameful indentured servitude-type treatment from the United States Soccer Federation.

Mocking the infamous plaintive cry of US champion figure skater Nancy Kerrigan after archrival American Tonya Harding's goons busted up her legs with a crowbar the day before the start of the 1994 US Figure Skating Championships *Why, Why, Why, Why????*

"Why" was the team unable to negotiate better compensation and so-called "lifestyle" benefits?

Answer: Leverage. Despite being World Cup and Olympic champions, the USWNT did *not* have any leverage.

And US Soccer knew it.

Still, leverage or no leverage, the champion USWNT's paltry earnings and other indignities foisted upon and courageously endured by these strong proud women while representing the United States of America was untenable.

World and Olympic champions being paid slave wages with no ancillary economic benefits just didn't sit right with me.

And by 2012, it didn't sit right with the players either.

The Cycle

Intuitively I wondered how the US Soccer Federation was able to continue to pay the USWNT slave wages year after year after year. Notwithstanding Langel's experience representing employers in CBA situations, he was certainly skilled enough to get more money for the employees.

So, why didn't it happen?

Well, just like I told the players before they hired me, they hold the control, and they must empower me to get them what they want. I am only as powerful as the power they give me to fight for them.

The situation transported me back to the year 1979 when, as a world-class track and field competitor and one of the athlete leaders, I helped fight for respect, and a percentage of the revenues and fair representation and the ability to vote on all matters impacting track athletes governed by The Athletics Congress (TAC)—the newly formed National

Governing Body (NGB) of track and field in the United States. Needless to say, we were not embraced by the powers that be at the TAC. Per the now famous and liberating 1978 Ted Stevens Act, Congress dismantled the Olympic sport cartel known as the Amateur Athletic Union—the AAU—and created twenty-four separate national governing bodies of amateur sport. The Athletic Congress governed track and field. And the United States Soccer Federation controlled soccer.

Notwithstanding the congressional dismantling of the AAU cartel, the same autocratic leaders that controlled each sport under the AAU umbrella emerged to control their sports under their respective new NGB entity. Essentially, the autonomy of the twenty-four national governing bodies actually made each entity more powerful than they had been in the AAU, and relegated their respective athletes to even more oppression.

To make sure democratic governance prevailed within each NGB, the Ted Stevens Act empowered the United States Olympic Committee to oversee and govern the operations of each NGB, supposedly to ensure that each one followed the rules of existence promulgated by the ACT. Almost fifty years after the empowerment of the NGBs and the USOC's governing oversight of the NGBs, the sordid histories of the mistreatment, and in many instances, crimes perpetrated against female Olympic athletes by these NGB—US Gymnastics, US Figure Skating, US Taekwondo, and the US Soccer Federation—all under the blind eye of the complicit USOC overseer is legendary. Accordingly, it is abundantly clear that all Olympic athletes, especially female competitors, need extremely strong athlete leadership to fight their indignant, abusive NGBs.

My firsthand experiences while still an active competitor leading track and field athletes that included star competitors Edwin Moses, the late Harvey Glance, Rose Monday, Willie Banks, Renaldo Nehemiah, Doriane Lambelet-Coleman and others prepared me to represent the USWNT in their modern-day fight for equality and respect. Almost half-a-century has passed, but the basic battles against NGBs remained the same. In a sense, the NGBs in every sport prevail because the "cycle" weeds out the veteran athletes who, if they can hang on and endure the outrageous indignities, can coalesce and mount a united fight against powerful NGBs and their mighty, complicit overseer, the USOC, now the USOPC.

The down and dirty fight for basic rights of representation in the sport of track and field against the TAC (now known as USA Track & Field) certainly convinced me that the athletes had to empower their internal and external leaders to fight the NGB juggernauts. Being totally unified in the fight and transferring that unity to their leadership was the only way to create power and leverage.

Despite many positive changes in track and field, in December 1991, after a fourteen-year-long battle with the TAC (1978 to 1991), as a result of attrition, and the slow but steady erosion of our unified veterans, coupled with the institutional staying power of the TAC, the power of my generation of athletes on the US track team was snuffed out. A new crop of young, bright-eyed, naïve, "just happy to be here" athletes comprised the majority and the power of unity was neutralized.

At that time, I was the vice chairperson of the Athletes Advisory Committee (AAC). The chairperson had resigned before our annual TAC Convention at which the NGB's power, politics, and economics were sorted out. The executive director of the TAC, Ollan Cassell, was a powerful, very smart, savvy, and skilled Donald Trump–type political figure who somehow bobbed and weaved his way through seemingly death-defying situations.

Having been stripped of any semblance of power due to the passage of time's dismantling of my veteran athlete power base, I knew this was my last convention, and Cassell knew it too.

A few minutes before I called to order the last of the AAC general meetings over which I'd preside, Cassell approached me, putting his arm around my shoulder. At this point, it was the end of our fourteen years of battle as enemies, and he said, "Rich, nothing personal ... this has all been politics."

His gesture was a show of respect. It was an acknowledgement that we as track athletes in search of self-determination inside of an organization that we knew would do anything to protect their omnipotence, that despite our knowledge of that stark reality, and absent physical and financial resources, we were unified and persevered as a formidable unit for more than a decade in search of equality.

Along the way, we did have some significant victories—establishing the stringent Olympic in-competition and out-of-competition drug testing protocols being the most significant—and for me, Cassell's respectful gesture in my waning moments of presence in the TAC was a sincere acknowledgment of the battles we waged as a unified entity with the powers that be.

Accordingly, from my perch of real "in their shoes" experience, I told the team that if they want something from US Soccer, the twenty-four players on the team have to be totally unified 24-0 in their resolve and their commitment. Otherwise I would have no power to get them what they want in a negotiation.

In short, the players had to create *leverage*. Unity gave the players leverage.

Simply stated, if the USWNT wanted better compensation, they could get it if players were unified, and it had to be UNANIMOUS!

Unanimous equals POWER!

Langel knew that.

US Soccer knew that.

But the players didn't know that.

As 2000, 2004, and 2008 came and went, the makeup of the team shifted. Partly because of the terrible compensation and partly because of injuries and attrition. Rarely did players stay on the team more than four to six years. As a result, there was a constant influx of new players on the team and a rotation of older players off of the team. The Cycle.

It was the same cycle I experienced decades ago in track and field.

Unbeknownst to the players, the cycle caused them to not create the unified bond required to create leverage. Notwithstanding the players' unwitting blindness to the potential power that could be derived from their unity, the US Soccer Federation was most certainly aware of the potential powder keg.

Certainly, to the delight of the USSF, seasoned and more economically astute *we need more money* veterans leave the team. Young, *I'm happy to be here and will do and endure anything to be on the US Team* players filled USWNT spots left behind by veterans.

As it happened and not necessarily by design, as players were reaching the tenure and a level of maturity on the team where they would come to the realization that playing for the USWNT was their profession, they naturally became more aware of and uncomfortable with their paltry compensation, accommodations, and level of respect received from USSF compared to the men's team.

After about three to four years, the *"just happy to be on the team"* perspective and shine wore off. At that point in the USWNT membership cycle, the more mature professional players began to question their socioeconomic status and value in the US Soccer ecosystem.

Importantly, if the majority of the players were young, and the *"just happy to be on the team"* mentality prevailed, the older players would not be able to build a foundation of veteran players strong enough to create the unity and leverage (e.g. threaten strike or boycott) required to make demands of the federation for better compensation through CBA negotiations or otherwise.

So, absent a majority of seasoned veteran players, and therefore no opportunity to create leverage via longevity, the older players would quietly cycle off the team.

This same cycle phenomenon extinguished the power of track and field athletes in 1991 … and thirty-two years later, they have yet to reengage their power. Their federation—now the USATF—just waited them out.

But, between 2004 and 2012, due to their cohesiveness—a characteristic borne of the great taste of success through perennial unbeaten streaks of the 2008 and 2012 Olympic gold medals and second-place finish in the 2011 World Cup—older players did not cycle off of the team. Instead, in late 2012, Olympic gold in hand, these seasoned, ever-more astute and savvy players recognized their bond, cohesive sense of purpose on the pitch, and total commitment to excellence, and decided to transfer that resolve to their demand for higher compensation.

US Soccer must have been surprised with the newfound strength of the USWNT. In their 2012 CBA negotiations, the players demanded more money and better overall terms.

The "Pay-to-Play" System

Every time the team requested equal pay at the outset of their CBA negotiations in 2000, 2004, and 2008, the federation responded by offering the team the total 100 percent bonus, so-called pay-to-play system utilized to compensate the US Soccer Men's Team.

Until the 2022 CBA, the USWNT players *always* rejected the pay-to-play (PTP) compensation system.

Because, simply it was *not* equal pay.

PTP was essentially the vehicle utilized by US Soccer to pay the men. Since the top male players would rather play for their international professional teams than take the time off from earning big money from their lucrative professional engagements to play for the US team, US Soccer had to incentivize the men to play for them. Thus, the federation created the PTP total bonus compensation system that by 2014 paid each of the USMNT Players $17,625 to play and win a game for the US Team.

Contrary to popular belief, the USWNT's 2022 adoption of the PTP system did *not* deliver equal pay to the USWNT. PTP was and remains a *system* by which the USSF distributes compensation to the USMNT. Importantly, as with the operation and outcomes of the execution of any system, the devil is in the details. US Soccer's pay-to-play system is no exception.

Whether or not the USWNT would receive the same amount of compensation as the men's team via invocation of the PTP system was totally contingent on (a) the number of games US Soccer schedules for the men's and women's teams, (b) win/loss/tie outcomes of those games, and (c) FIFA world ranking of each opponent. In short, if the USWNT and USMNT were scheduled to play the same number of games each year, against teams of similar FIFA world ranking, *then and only then* would the women be positioned to *possibly* earn equal pay. If not, the teams would not get equal pay. It's that simple.

More importantly, unlike the USWNT, since playing for the USMNT was not their primary source of income, the players on the men's team could literally afford to take the risk of being paid (or not) per game scheduled by the federation via the PTP 100 percent bonus system. The compensation matrix of the PTP system in which US Soccer controlled the identity of the opponent, scheduling of games and through the operation of this PTP system, whether or not the men's team would earn income is a very risky system indeed. Unlike the USWNT players, the players on the USMNT did not need the money to survive, so they could therefore afford to take the PTP risk.

Contrarily, playing for the USWNT was the women's *only* source of income. Succinctly stated, the USWNT players could not withstand the very real PTP risk of having no income.

Given the history of US Soccer's policy of a USWNT marketing and promotion dark period following the USWNT's World Cup and Olympic triumphs, coupled with US Soccer's counterintuitive scheduling of fewer games for the USWNT at the height of the team's popularity, the women on the USWNT could not agree to accept the PTP compensation system and take the risk of the federation not scheduling any games for them.

No games scheduled equals no income for the USWNT.

Accordingly, absent a guarantee from the federation that they would schedule games, or at best, a TBD minimum number of games per year for the USWNT so that the team would have a predictable base and minimum level of annual income—there was no way the USWNT could ever consider adopting the PTP compensation system.

And to be clear, during CBA negotiations in 2016, the federation emphatically proclaimed that they would *never* guarantee the scheduling of games. *Not ever!*

Notably, per the terms of the new 2022 CBA, US Soccer is obligated to schedule a minimum of thirteen games for the women's team. But, importantly, in the pay-to-play compensation system, unlike the last twenty-years, USWNT players are not under contract to play for the USWNT for a set amount of annual income. Instead, the amount of money a USWNT player will earn each year is uncertain and dependent on three variables—two of which are controlled solely by US Soccer.

First, US Soccer has to select and call-up a player to play a game for the USWNT. So, even though the federation is contractually obligated to schedule a minimum of thirteen USWNT games each year, the number of games a USWNT player plays each year is totally up to the discretion of the federation. As a result, the players' ability to earn income is uncertain. So, like the men on the USMNT, the pay-to-play system provides them an equal opportunity to not earn any income at all.

Next, the minimum amount of money to be earned by the USWNT players who are fortunate enough to be called up to play a game for the USWNT is $8,000 per game. But, the maximum amount of bonus money to be earned per game is dependent on two variables– the opponent selected by US Soccer, and the FIFA world ranking of that opponent.

Finally, the maximum amount of money each USWNT player called up to play a game will earn is dependent upon whether or not the USWNT wins, loses, or plays to a draw, and the FIFA world ranking of the opponent. Accordingly, in the pay-to-play compensation system, the annual maximum/minimum income a USWNT player lucky enough to be called up for all thirteen games the federation is obligated to schedule is $8,000 per game or a total of $104,000. The fewer games that are played by a USWNT player, the less money she will earn. And, since playing for the USWNT is each players' primary source of income, unlike the men on the USMNT who enjoy primary income from their lucrative international club team employment, each USWNT player will live a life of income insecurity.

The fact is, by adopting the PTP system of compensation, the USWNT—like the USMNT—has accepted the equal opportunity to have no games scheduled by US Soccer, and therefore earn zero income from the Federation.

A true, real, shameful false equivalence sold to the USWNT and the world as equal pay.

In truth, it's an equal opportunity for the USWNT to not get paid at all.

PART II

5

Tactic I: Building Leverage: The Initial Establishment of Team Unanimity and Leverage

MY DUTIES AS the executive director of the Women's National Team Players Association (USWNTPA), the official collective bargaining unit for the USWNT, began on January 1 of 2015. John Langel was the previous executive director and general counsel to represent the players for fourteen years. Over that time, the US Soccer Federation developed a close bond with Langel. Specifically, the longtime president of US Soccer, Sunil Gulati, and Langel had struck up a cordial friendship. As a result, some players became concerned that maybe their relationship was too cozy.

I knew that from the onset I was going to have to disabuse Gulati and US Soccer of any notion that I was a novice so they could eliminate any thoughts of *influencing* me. So, I arranged an introductory call in December 2014 with Gulati, Dan Flynn (CEO of US Soccer), and Lisa

Levine (general counsel of US Soccer). The purpose of the call was to be direct with US Soccer. I wanted to let them know who I was and what I was about. At that point, I had been a sports lawyer for more than thirty years, and there wasn't anything in sports I had not done. I had competed internationally as a member of the US track & field team, been an executive in a professional sports league, run sports teams, represented players, coaches, sports entities, and assisted in negotiating corporate sponsorship and television broadcast agreements. Notably, I had practiced law in the venture capital space through the startup technology company world of Silicon Valley, considered myself an expert in sports law, and was also quite candid about the fact that I was not a pushover and didn't take any crap from anybody.

Additionally, I let them know that I was going to be pushing back on a lot of the madness that they had thrown at this team during my predecessor's reign as executive director of the players association. I was the new sheriff in town.

I knew little about negotiating collective-bargaining agreements. Since the memorandum of understanding (MOU)—essentially the incomplete collective bargaining agreement that governed the relationship between the USWNT and US Soccer—was set to expire in December 2016, I knew that I was going to need to find an expert in collective bargaining negotiations in sports to help me in this regard. So, in October 2014 right after I signed the agreement to represent the women's national team, I reached out to an old friend, Arthur McAfee, who served as senior counsel to the NFL Players Association for more than seventeen years.

I had coffee with McAfee at the Caribou coffee shop on 17th Street in Washington, DC, not too far from the White House and told him what had transpired and what I was planning to do with the USWNT. I presented him with an opportunity to assist me with the challenges that I faced as the executive director and general counsel for the women's national soccer team, but there was one caveat. McAfee would not be compensated for the first year of his assistance because the Players Association had no money. Without hesitation and to my surprise, McAfee replied, "I'm in."

Needless to say, I was relieved. I had a partner who had lived through the real battles of collective bargaining in sports, a lawyer who had worked alongside Gene Upshaw, the visionary executive director of the NFL Players Association. Upshaw battled the NFL for many years and came out the other end with massive compensation and a plethora of other benefits for his clients. One of the key economic platforms that Upshaw had created for the NFLPA was a creative group licensing plan (GLP) that continues to heap millions of dollars into the pockets of each and every NFL player. My plan was to ask McAfee to create a similar GLP for the USWNT. To this day, in my view, every professional athlete in football, baseball, basketball, and hockey has Gene Upshaw and his trusty lawyer Arthur McAfee to thank for hanging in there and fighting for players' rights to be compensated fairly.

So, in January 2015, I jumped in the saddle and immediately began to push back on US Soccer and some of the craziness they continued to shove on the US women's soccer team.

By mid-January, Lisa Levine approached me with a deal that the federation was pursuing with EA Sports, a massive video game manufacturer that made billions of dollars through the likes of games such as Madden, FIFA, PGA Tour, UFC, and others.

At that time, EA Sports had a game titled *FIFA 15*, which surprisingly featured the United States men's soccer team. After all, the US men's team had a history of lackluster performances in the World Cup and the Olympic Games. However, I imagined that the American market for video games was such that it made sense for EA Sports to have a soccer game to sell to the young American male.

Lisa called me and told me that US Soccer was renegotiating its deal with EA Sports and they wanted to feature the women's national team in their next game, which would be entitled *FIFA 16*. Additionally, she told me that for the first four years of the EA Sports deal, the men were paid $120,000 per year, for a total of $480,000, all of which monies accrued to the Men's National Soccer Team Players Association. For *FIFA 16*, Lisa told me that EA Sports wanted to feature the women's national soccer team and that they also wanted a star female player to do a cover for the game. So, I asked, "Great, how much money are we talking?"

Incredulously, Lisa told me that EA Sports was *not* going to pay the women any money for their appearance in the FIFA 2016 game. NO COMPENSATION FOR THE USWNT!!

Instead of monetary compensation, Levine stated that the federation thought that this would be a great awareness and marketing opportunity for the women's national team and they should do it for free.

I laughed and told her you can't be serious. Levine said she was very serious. So, I laughed again. After all, the women didn't need any more awareness. The world already knew about the perennial Olympic and World Cup–champion US National Women's Soccer Team. They already were aware of the plethora of star players that include Hope Solo, Alex Morgan, Abby Wambach, and others who were on the women's national team. It's the men's national team that the world did not know or care about. Why should the women's team be featured in the *FIFA 16* game where the men get paid and the women's team do not get paid?

Per my obligation as executive director of the players association, I relayed the offer to the team and they rejected it out of hand. I told Lisa that the team said no. They were not going to do the deal without getting paid. Lisa said there would be no deal and I said that was fine with us.

A couple of days later, Lisa called me and asked whether or not the team would accept a nominal payment for their participation in the *FIFA 16* game. She told me that EA Sports had already completed the promotional markup for the game and that it would be quite expensive to go back and delete any reference to the women's national team in the game. She also said that they already decided to feature a star player from the women's national team on the cover of the game. But she said that she understood that the team needed to be compensated for their involvement and since the deal was really just a two-year renewal of the men's deal with EA Sports, the men would still be paid $120,000 per year ($240,000 total) and the United States Soccer Federation was willing to pay the women's team $10,000 per year ($20,000 total) for their participation in the *FIFA 16* game. Essentially, the US Soccer Federation had promised the women's participation, but they couldn't deliver the USWNT to EA Sports. In order to keep their deal and, I surmised, not breach their contract with EA Sports, the Federation had to offer the women's national team some money to be part of the game.

I told Lisa that I would take the offer back to the team. The team decided to accept the $20,000. By demanding and ultimately receiving compensation from the federation, the USWNT made it absolutely clear to US Soccer that the federation could no longer deliver the name, image, and likeness of US Women's National Soccer Team to any corporate sponsor for without paying the players. It was as a huge, precedent-setting victory for the USWNT.

The USWNT's *free* days were over.

I had hoped that by pushing back we communicated to the federation that the team was no longer going to work for free. I thought it would send a message to the federation that the next time they approach us with a deal, there had better be some significant financial compensation attached to it for the players.

But to the surprise of nobody, that was not going to be the case.

***

HOPE SPRINGS ETERNAL. I soon realized that it was going to take more than pushing back on one deal for US Soccer to get the message that their twenty-year history of pimping these women for free were over. Between February 2015 and the beginning of the World Cup in June 2015, the US Soccer Federation continually approached the US women's national team with endorsement sponsorship deals. The common dominator was that the USWNT was always offered either no compensation or relative chump change to participate in a US Soccer sponsor promotion or advertisement campaign.

The most egregious example of US Soccer's attempted exploitation of the USWNT was a proposed Budweiser-sponsored television series, a documentary that would follow the US women's soccer team twenty-four hours a day, seven days a week in the months leading up to the 2015 World Cup. It was the equivalent of the famous *Hard Knocks* reality sports documentary television series produced by NFL Films and broadcast on HBO. The federation had offered the USWNT 24/7 series opportunity to Fox Television, and Fox secured Budweiser to sponsor and finance the venture. The USWNT was not consulted with regard to participation, nor were they offered a penny for their prospective participation in what would be a very intrusive production.

The team was incensed when I told them about the deal. "Absolutely NOT" was their unequivocal, unanimous response to the offer.

When I told Lisa Levine the Team declined and would not participate, again, she told me that the Federation had a contract with Fox and Budweiser committing the team to the production. Once again, I informed Levine that the Federation did not have the right to commit the USWNT to any deals without consulting with the players. And that further, committing them to a 24/7 video camera in their face, their hotel room, the locker room, and the bedroom was a bit over the top. Clearly, there were huge privacy concerns. Further, it was outrageous to think that even if they agreed to participate, they would do it for free!

At this point, Lisa asked me how much money would it take to get the Team to participate. Wisely, the player representatives Abby Wambach, Christie Rampone, and Hope Solo suggested that one of them should have a call with the USSF, Fox, and Budweiser representatives and listen to their pitch. Abby was selected to be on the call with me.

Fox, Budweiser, and the USSF were excited and openly welcomed the call with me and Abby. They thought they'd be able to "pitch" it and convince Abby that it is a great opportunity for the team. The call was scheduled for 1:00 p.m. Pacific Time on a Sunday afternoon. When the call commenced, Abby informed us that she had a hard stop at 2:00 p.m. PT.

Fox began by noting that the theme and objective of the production was to showcase each member of the team individually and collectively—24/7—in order to make their fans feel like they really knew them and had a personal relationship with the team.

About thirty minutes in to the Fox executives' presentation, Abby abruptly interrupted him and said, *Hey, I really hate to interrupt, but I just arrived here in LA and have some things I really need to do this afternoon, so let's just cut to the chase. This sounds like a very intrusive production and for our team to even begin to think about participating, you are* *going to have to pay us $200,000. That's our number. If you can't pay it, we are not participating. So, thank you all for your time. I'll leave the rest of this call to Rich.*

And with that $200,000 demand, Abby left. Silence was all that remained. About one week later, Levine told me that they might attempt to produce the show anyway by leveraging the players' "media availability" obligations. I shot her down immediately by noting that the players would simply not show up for non-game media avails. After that, I never heard about it again.

The next deal US Soccer tried to push on the women's team leading up to the 2015 World Cup was a deal with Chevrolet that would require the participation of ten players from the women's national soccer team. Each would be paid $2,000 to participate in a four-month-long, interactive social media–based promotional commercial advertisement endorsing a partnership between US Soccer and Chevrolet. In essence, the federation was offering the USWNT an exclusive World Cup–related automotive product category endorsement deal that would net ten players $2,000 each for a total of $20,000. The exclusivity of the deal would prohibit the US Women's National Team Players Association (USWNTPA) and each of its players from doing a separate individual endorsement of any other automotive company.

That was $2,000 to a player to give countless hours of time to film commercial spots, a commitment to be available for social media interaction with fans, and no way of earning money for other car deals. That was going to be a hard no from the women's soccer team.

We counteroffered and requested $120,000 to be paid to six players in this deal, with each player getting $20,000. Not to our surprise, the federation rejected our counteroffer. As a result, we walked away with no deal.

The next opportunity presented to the women's national team by the US Soccer Federation was a deal with TAG Heuer, the exclusive Swiss high-end watch company. The federation wanted the team to endorse TAG's great product, but like so many other deals, the federation did not want to pay the women's national team for the association. Not surprisingly, the women said no.

Interestingly, shortly after we rejected participation in the promotion, Alex Morgan, a star player of the team who had already appeared in official US Soccer photos announcing TAG's deal with US Soccer, told the team that she had discussions with the president of TAG Heuer, and that they really wanted the women's team to participate. If the team did decide to participate, each player would receive a $10,000 watch in exchange for partaking. US Soccer had already inked a federation sponsorship deal with TAG and unbeknownst to us, TAG had asked the federation if Morgan could be the USWNT's representative endorser.

The players association still rejected the opportunity. In an attempt to force the players to participate in the TAG promotions, US Soccer invoked what they claimed to be the federation's right (supposedly delineated in the 2013 MOU) to sell the image of likeness of the team and the players to a federation sponsor (e.g. TAG Heuer) via the group licensing provisions of the expired 2012 collective agreement, and the still-active standard player agreements. Incensed, we objected to US Soccer's ridiculous assertion of unfettered rights to the name, image, and likeness (NIL) of each and every player on the team, so US Soccer filed a grievance stating that the MOU and the standard player agreement did provide US Soccer those rights.

The filing of the TAG grievance represented the first official legal battle with US Soccer in which the USWNT challenged the legitimacy and efficacy of the MOU that I inherited. More importantly, it was the first time that I was seeing firsthand what Hope Solo had warned me about earlier. The federation invoked classic divide and conquer tactics by selecting and thereby hopefully currying favor with certain players to whom endorsement deals would be offered by the federation in order to get those players to convince the team to do things they might not otherwise do.

By April 2015, the USWNT players had, for the first time in at least fourteen years, pushed back on US Soccer and effectively thwarted and refused to participate in four major endorsement opportunities in which US Soccer had, without the players' knowledge, participation, or assent, sold them to US Soccer sponsors to commercially exploit without any compensation. They did so by forcefully, effectively, and consistently pushing back on the federation's pimping of the players to

EA Sports, Fox, Budweiser, Chevrolet, and TAG Heuer—all "A-list" corporate sponsors—denying the federation and these companies the opportunity to exploit the names, images, and likeness of the soon-to-be World Cup champions without paying the players for their participation. For the first time since 1999, the players had invoked the power of unity, thereby creating the leverage they needed to push US Soccer for bigger, more meaningful concessions … like equal pay.

Divide, conquer, and compensate. These tried-and-true tactics, masterfully invoked by US Soccer over the years, failed with the 2015 version of the USWNT, but don't be fooled. At the first sign of a crack in the players' armor, US Soccer was always ready to redeploy, divide, conquer, and compensate.

We're Not Playing, Rich. Fuck them, we're not playing. Just tell them that we're not playing. That's what I heard at 8:15 a.m. Central Time on July 10, 2015, on a call from Christie Rampone, the captain of the USWNT. It was only five days after their World Cup victory that captured the hearts and minds of Americans all over the country. While Rampone talked with me, the team was on their way from the midtown Manhattan set of *Good Morning America* to the beginning of the ticker tape parade in lower Manhattan's "Canyon of Heroes" to celebrate their title.

Just a few days earlier on the morning after the team's World Cup victory, Sunil Gulati called captains Abby Wambach and Christie Rampone to tell them that the team's request for the weekend off was denied, and they were all going to be forced to play their National Women's Soccer League (NWSL) games that coming weekend. Unbeknownst to me, Abby and Christie, on behalf of the team, had asked Gulati for the weekend off. They did not have the energy to play the NWSL games scheduled in various cities just five days after their exhausting World Cup journey.

Essentially after a grueling thirty-day, World Cup tournament in Canada, the players were physically, mentally, and emotionally spent and did not want to play in their professional games that coming weekend. Their request was vociferously denied by Gulati and the US Soccer Federation. Abby and Christie decided they would wait one more day and reissue their request the next morning, two days after the

World Cup championship game. Surely, Gulati would exhibit some compassion and grant their modest request … right? No such luck.

As recounted to me by Rampone, the response from Gulati was immediate.

Emphatically, Gulati told Rampone that the players had to play those NWSL games that coming weekend. He noted that all of the NWSL teams had developed huge marketing and promotional campaigns around the World Cup–champion USWNT to sell out their respective stadiums that weekend, and that he didn't care how the players were feeling, that no matter what, they were going to play.

For emphasis, and to drive home this point, Gulati continued, that in order to make sure that the entire team understood it, he would convene a conference call Wednesday night with the entire team and tell them all that unequivocally they will be playing in their NWSL games that weekend! That's when Christie called me. They had hoped to keep me out of the situation. They thought their reasonable request would be summarily granted. Rampone made it clear to me that they did not want to play and that they had no interest in a conference call with Sunil the following night to talk about it. Immediately, I told Christie that under no circumstances would the team participate in a conference call with him. Technically, Gulati's issuance of a conference call demand without consulting the players association (me) first was an unfair labor practice, and he knew it.

For at least twelve years during his reign as president of the federation, Sunil had always operated this way. Players told me he always called players to intimidate, make demands, issue ultimatums, and veiled threats of expulsion or exclusion from the USWNT if players did not comply with his wishes. Notwithstanding labor laws prohibiting Gulati from unilateral contact with any of the players, he always ignored the technicalities and according to several players, reached out to them to intimidate, or do whatever else he had to do to get his way.

This was classic Sunil Gulati, The King (as I liked to call him), behavior. However, this time around, he had to deal with me. I told Christie I would make sure that Sunil would talk to me, and I would make sure that the Gulati-mandated team call would be canceled. If he or anyone else at the federation still wanted to address the team, they were obliged per law to talk to me, the Players Association executive director. So, I picked up the phone and called the US Soccer's general Counsel Lisa Levine.

By July 2015, I had developed a pretty good relationship with Lisa. I told her that if Sunil wanted to talk to somebody about the team's schedule for the rest of this "World Cup Championship Celebration" week, he would have to talk to me. After all, I'm the executive director of the players association and by law, any request made by management to employees has to be made through the executive director of the players union. She agreed and scheduled a call for the following night between me, her, and Dan Flynn, the CEO of US Soccer. As usual, Sunil never participated in tough meetings or calls. He always sent Dan.

At approximately 6:30 p.m. Central Time on July 8, the call took place. I politely listened to Dan lecture me and tell me what the players were going to be doing over the course of the next few days. In other words, he told me what the players' post–World Cup victory schedule was going to look like between Wednesday and Saturday … with an unmistakable, *whether the players liked it or not* attitude. He said that the team would be flown from Chicago to Los Angeles on Thursday for some West Coast celebrations. Then, the team would be on a redeye Thursday night on Southwest Airlines from Los Angeles to New York City where early on Friday morning the team would appear on the *Today* show, followed by a trip to the studios of *Good Morning America*. The team would then be transported by bus to the start of the ticker-tape parade in lower Manhattan. After the parade and honorary luncheon with New York City Mayor Bill de Blasio, the team would be dispersed to their respective NWSL games that weekend, and that was that.

When Flynn's lecture ended, I thanked him for the information and told him I would get back to him to let him know what the players were going to do. Sounding flabbergasted, he asked, *What do you mean let us know what they're going to do? I* repeated what I'd said. It was as if the call was cut off, but I could still hear breathing on the other side of the call. And with that, I could hear a click and the call was over.

Later that evening, I sat down at the computer and drafted an email to the team. I told them about Flynn's lecture and what he definitively dictated would be their schedule over the next few days. I told the newly crowned World Cup champion USWNT that the schedule included playing in their respective NWSL games that coming weekend with no exceptions. I asked the team to carefully review this email, including the dictated schedule, and if they didn't want to do anything in that schedule, including playing those NWSL games, they should just let me know.

But, my proviso was that if they did not want to do anything in that schedule—most specifically, if they did not want to play in those NWSL games that coming weekend—they needed complete unanimity. Unanimous meant leveraging their World Cup championship into the *power* to determine their future.

As the team exited the studios a few days later, they boarded their luxury bus and made sure that no US Soccer officials were on the vehicle that would transport them to the start of the ticker-tape parade in lower Manhattan. I picked up the phone and I could hear and feel the raucous, almost jubilant energy in the background. "We're not playing, Rich. Tell him [Gulati] we're not playing. Fuck him. We're not playing. We are tired and we're gonna do what we want to do". And with that, with much glee and hyperbole, Christie said, "Well Rich, I guess you can hear it. The team has voted twenty-four to nothing to not play the games this weekend. Let US Soccer know and then let us know what they have to say." I told Christie that was a great, courageous decision, and the unanimous vote was *powerful*. I knew it was an absolutely powerful by-product of winning the World Cup.

Winners amass power. Power provides winners the leverage required to get what they want. The USWNT was about to utilize that leverage to get something they wanted, which was a weekend off. It may not look like a huge deal, but these were the small hurdles that one must overcome to establish a fair negotiation tactic. *Leverage*.

I told Christie that I would immediately draft a letter to US Soccer informing them of their decision to not play the NWSL games and email the draft letter to each one of them so they could review it and approve it. Subsequently, later that afternoon when all US Soccer officials were no longer physically with, or able to physically access or in any way influence the players, I would forward the letter to Lisa Levine, the general counsel; Dan Flynn, the CEO; and Sunil Gulati, the president of US Soccer, informing them that the players were not going to take part in their NWSL pro games that weekend. I drafted the letter as I watched the team's ticker-tape parade live on CNN. I emailed the letter to the players and it appeared that some of the players were reading the letter on their phones as they rode the float through the ticker-tape parade in lower Manhattan's Canyon of Heroes. Just before the parade concluded, the players approved the letter and at about 3:00 p.m., I sent it to US Soccer and the battle began.

Lisa called me almost immediately, even though she was on vacation in Europe. She couldn't believe what she was reading. "What is this? What are you telling me in this letter, Rich?" she said incredulously.

"Lisa, I think you can read English. It says what it says," I told her calmly. "It says that the World Cup champions are physically, mentally, and emotionally fatigued after a thirty-day, grueling World Cup championship journey in Canada and they are not going to play in the scheduled NWSL games this coming weekend." "What do you mean?" Lisa said again. "Lisa, exactly what the letter says," I repeated. "But … you can't do that," Lisa said in disbelief. "Yes they can," I said. "And they are not playing this weekend." "We're going to get on a call with Dan Flynn," Lisa retorted. I said, "Fine, let me know when." About half an hour later, Dan called me with Lisa on the phone. "Rich, what is this?" Dan asked.

I said matter of factly, "Dan, as I told Lisa in plain English, it is what it is. It's a letter notifying you that the team is physically, mentally, and emotionally exhausted and they're not playing the NWSL pro games this weekend." Flynn regurgitated Lisa's reaction—"But, you can't do that." "We just did," I replied. "But … you guys, the players have contracts and are obligated to play," Lisa explained.

Dan immediately responded to Lisa's legal challenge to our mini-work stoppage by saying, "I don't want to get involved in a legal argument right now. This is a business decision. Let's not talk about legalities." I don't know if he knew it or not, but Dan's momentary avoidance of haggling over whether or not the players were contractually obliged to play NWSL games was a wise choice because the ace card I had in my back pocket was the product of an incredible blunder perpetrated for twenty-plus years by an overconfident, brash US Soccer Federation.

The USWNT players had never signed contracts to play for the USWNT … and they definitely had not signed contracts to play for the NWSL. So, legally, the players did not have any obligation to play for the USWNT or the NWSL. "Rich, what's it gonna take for the team to play?" Dan asked in a disgusted tone.

I replied, "I don't know what it's gonna take for them to play."

Dan said, "You have a decision to make. You tell me what is it going take for them to play."

I countered, "The team makes their decisions, then they inform me of what their decisions are, and then I inform you. I don't dictate to them what they're going to do. The players tell me what they're going do, and then I tell you what they are going to do, and they told me to tell you they're not playing this weekend."

"Well, there's gotta be something they want. Is it money?" Dan asked with exasperation.

I said, "I don't know but, I'll go back and ask them. Let's talk in an hour." So, that's what I did. I told Christie they're offering money. Christie asked me, "How much do you think we should ask for?" I suggested asking for $10,000 for each of our twenty-four players for a total of $240,000. Further, we will tell them we will take $240,000 to appear at the NWSL games this weekend, but we're not going to play the games. We will simply appear and sign autographs. Christie loved that proposal.

So at the appointed time, I called Dan and Lisa back and offered the counter as discussed with Christie. "That's a nonstarter!" Dan blurted out, "That's a nonstarter!"

So I replied, "Well then, this discussion is over. It was good talking to you."

"What do you mean this discussion is over?" a flustered Dan exclaimed.

"Look, Dan, I told you guys way back in December 2014 before I took over the players association that I don't play games. My words are my tools. In my world, words are my weapons and when someone tells me that something is a nonstarter that means there's nothing to talk about—so, see you later," I said matter of factly.

"Bad choice of words on my part," Dan said regretfully. "I'm sorry for the choice of words. I need to take that proposal back to Sunil and the board and I'll get back to you in an hour." When Flynn and Levine called back, their message was bizarre.

"The USSF board rejects your $240,000 demand, but as a counter, they offer to donate $100,000 to New York City mayor de Blasio's favorite charity in the name of the US Women's National Soccer Team," Dan announced. I didn't know what to make of that offer. To be honest, I thought it was kind of crazy. But I had a job to do and take it back to the players.

Christie laughed uproariously when I told her about US Soccer's counter. "That's a crazy offer," said Christie. "It's rejected. We want our money, Rich." I called Dan and Lisa back and told them the $100,000 charity offer was rejected. It was going to be $10,000 per player or the players would be no-shows at the upcoming weekend NWSL games. At this juncture, Lisa was compelled to wield what she erroneously believed to be her "legal leverage."

"If they don't play this weekend, the players will be in violation of their contracts, they will be in breach. So, by contract, the players are obligated to play—anything less than playing will be a breach of contract," Lisa said defiantly.

Dan Flynn noted again that he did not need to get into any legal entanglements. "This is a business issue. Let's solve the business problems first."

Dan didn't know it at the time, but he was actually being prescient. I had the ace card in my back pocket ... a card to be played only if it would reap unprecedented returns for the players. I believed the time was right to play the card. By playing the ace, not only would we prevail in getting $240,000 to appear and not play in that weekend's NWSL games, we would demonstrate to Dan, Lisa, Sunil, and the rest of the USSF board of directors that the players now had *all* of the power and *leverage* and could essentially take control and determine their destiny in the sport.

Essentially, I knew that Flynn and Levine had no idea that to my knowledge that never once in the history of the US Women's National Soccer Team—and certainly as it related to each of the twenty-four players on the 2015 team—never once had any player ever signed a standard player contract obligating them to play for the United States Women's National Soccer Team, or for the NWSL's pro league. Not once. Not ever. So, US Soccer did not have any signed contracts from any players to play. In essence, the players have no contractual obligation to play. And if they didn't play any games including games for the United States, they would not be in breach of contract. No contracts, no breach. That was my ace card, and if Lisa continued to push the breach of contract notion, I was ready to play.

"We have a problem," Dan said. "We can't agree. We need to think about this overnight." Okay, but let me be crystal clear," I replied. "We don't have a problem; you have a problem." Lisa couldn't resist and shot back, "No, Rich, you have a problem because the players will be in breach of contract." I said without hesitation, "You know, Lisa, that's the third time you said that tonight, and I didn't want to say this with your CEO on the line, but since you insist on injecting legal issues and brought it up three times I'm going to tell you that, there's no breach of contract because NONE of these players have ever signed a standard players agreement to play for the USA or to play for the NWSL, so you don't have any contracts signed by any players that they'd breach. ZERO contracts, with ZERO USWNT players, ZERO obligation to Play, ZERO," I said defiantly, "Z-E-R-O!"

Stunned, Dan said, "What?" We don't have any signed player contracts, Lisa?" Caught tremendously unprepared, Lisa stutters, "Well … well, we have a signed … a signed memorandum of under-standing (MOU) that obligates the players to play." I chuckled and said, "Lisa, you know as well as I do that the MOU … that flimsy incomplete 2013 MOU that is in essence a detailed term sheet that was never reduced to a definitive, official collective bargaining agree-ment (CBA), does not obligate any player to play. By definition, an MOU is an agreement to agree to terms of engagement between the players association and US Soccer. It is not an agreement that obli-gates any of the individual players to play for the USA or for the NWSL. So, as I stated, you have no contracts. The players are not contracted or obligated to play. You have no breach of contract." And with that, the phone call ended.

The next morning was a Saturday. My phone rang at 8 a.m., and Lisa's name came up on caller ID. I let the call go to voicemail. I wanted to hear the angst in her voicemail. I wanted to hear her now, for the first time, in a position of no control over the USWNT. "Rich, this is Lisa, please give us a call as soon as you get this message," she said anxiously. "We need to talk."

I waited an hour before I called back. When I called, Lisa patched Dan in. The tenor of the conversation was markedly different than it had been the night before. Both of them were deferential, respectful, even humbled. "Rich, I thought about what you said last night and there were two words that you mentioned several times that rang clearly in my ears. The first word was *commitment*. You said several times that US Soccer has never demonstrated the commitment to the women or the women's team that they deserve ... and you're right. We never really have," Flynn admitted. "The next word that stands out that you said over and over was that US Soccer has never shown any *respect* for the women's team, and I thought about that. I've concluded that you're right about that too."

Flynn sounded reflective and sincere, as he continued. "So, to demonstrate our commitment to the women's team and our utmost respect for the women's team, we're going to agree to pay $10,000 apiece to the fifteen players that will be playing NWSL games this weekend, for a total of $150,000, and we're also going to agree to provide $1.20 per ticket sold to every NWSL game this weekend at which a national team player plays to the USWNTPA Players Association. Is there anything else that you would like, or want?"

I told Dan that I appreciated the kind words and generous offer and I'd take it back to the players. But I told him that if there's anything else that we—the players and the players association—would want going forward, I would hope that we would receive sincere communication from the federation. I called Christie and told her about the deal. She quickly accepted on behalf of the players. Lisa and I agreed to the language in a hastily drafted agreement to duly memorialize our resolution. By 1:00 p.m., the players with NWSL games that night boarded their New York City flights and traveled to their respective game venues.

The team didn't realize it at the time, but with that show of force and resolve to not play NWSL games that weekend, the team had validated their power. By standing firm and *unanimously* agreeing to not work those NWSL games that weekend because they didn't want to, the players established their power base. Their unanimity established *leverage*. It established the power required to move forward and demand equal pay in the next collective bargaining agreement.

Effectively, the US women's national team had executed a threatened work stoppage—a boycott of NWSL games—in exchange for two days off work and a $340,000 premium ($150,000 to players, $190,000 ticket revenue to the players Association).

***

AT SOME POINT in early December 2015, the players refused to play the last of ten World Cup "Victory Tour" games in Hawaii. During the team's walk-through the day before the game in the stadium which at that time held the annual NFL Pro Bowl game, the players could not help but notice the rips, tears, and uneven seams of the terribly worn artificial turf.

I was in Texas on a Saturday afternoon when I received an emergency call from Hope Solo accompanied by an astonishing photo of the dangerous loose seam of the turf. An errant step on the field could potentially produce a serious injury—similar to the one experienced by Megan Rapinoe the previous week on a similar artificial turf surface at a Victory Tour practice facility.

On the spot, the players voted to boycott the game, which was scheduled to be nationally televised the next day. I called Lisa and Sunil to tell them the team would not be playing. I sent both of them the photo taken by Hope as evidence.

I asked Sunil if the federation had conducted a pregame inspection of the venue and condition of the playing surface before they selected the venue. Without hesitation, Sunil assured me that, as is USSF standard procedure, the venue had been inspected by the federation's Advance Team and the safety of the playing surface had been assured.

Sunil asked me to give him two hours to conduct some due diligence before I announced to the world that the team would not play the following day and were willing to forfeit the match. I agreed.

Lisa provided me updates every hour after the original two hours expired.

At about midnight central time, eight hours after my initial call with Sunil, Lisa called me to confirm that over the past few hours, the USSF had conducted its own inspection and agreed that the condition of the playing surface was in fact unacceptable. Accordingly, US Soccer would announce the cancellation of the next day's game.

Pure victory for the USWNT. Another powerful by-product of team unity.

It was December 2015, almost one year after the execution of our plan to push back on the unfettered, unchallenged edicts issued by the US Soccer Federation.

It appeared that we now had the leverage required to stake out our territory and push hard for equal pay in the upcoming CBA negotiations in January 2016.

During my entire two years as executive director of the USWNTPA, I only had two brief telephone conservations and one in-person solo interaction with Sunil. During these three encounters, he was polite, gracious, and almost humble. In the fourth and final exchange, which occurred at the one and only CBA negotiation session in which he personally participated in late October 2016, he was decidedly arrogant, lacking of humility, and very much the aggressive provocoteur many players had described him to be. At this point, he had flexed his muscles: fired Hope Solo, enlisted a few lesser "on the bubble" players to abandon equal pay and adopt the federation's "fair and equitable pay" camp, and had already scored significant points with the players in his quest to muzzle me (more on this in later chapters).

In his second call to me which occurred on the Sunday morning of the cancelled game, he did two things. First, he surprisingly admitted that in fact, the USSF's advance team had not inspected the playing surface and he apologized to the players through me for that potentially disastrous omission. He then asked me if we could be *on the same page* in our comments to the press about this matter.

I agreed to be on the same page, if the *words* on the page were true. He assured me that he and the federation would tell the full truth and take full responsibility.

He kept his word. The next day, the *New York Times* dedicated their "Sports Monday" front page to a comprehensive exposé of US Soccer's faux pax, a big mistake that not only could have resulted in physical disaster for players, but also exhibited front and center to the world that the federation *did not* have the same level of respect for the USWNT that it had for the USMNT. Without having to say it, everyone knew that the federation would certainly conduct a pregame inspection of a playing surface upon which the prized US Men's Team would play.

That is the power of unanimity. That is the power and commitment the players are required to accrue in order to effectively *leverage* something that has never been done before.

6

Tactic II: Nuclear Options

ANYONE WHO KNOWS me understands that I am an aggressive negotiator. In short, I do not ascribe to the academics who write books about negotiations and try to teach people about the psychology and finesse of negotiating.

Negotiation is *not* an academic exercise.

Negotiations are not sport or some finesse-laden art form.

Negotiation is WAR.

To be clear, I mean no disrespect to the negotiation "experts" out there, most of whom have never negotiated anything significant.

Academics describe a kumbaya sort of negotiation process, within which:

- Each side needs to understand the other side's personality,

- Each side needs to understand their opponent's tangible and intangible objectives,

- Each side needs to respect the opposing side and all other kinds of madness that in real life does not matter.

What does matter is how tough are you going to be in negotiating your side of the deal.

And when are you going to let the other side know that you plan to *go to the mattresses* in order to get what you want.

Most importantly, when you are in a David and Goliath situation negotiation—USWNT vs. the USSF—you need to let your opponent know right away that you're going to be tough, aggressive, and will take big risks.

Additionally, let them know that you have a nuclear option arsenal, and that you are more than willing to drop some nuclear bombs along the way to get what you want.

Drop the Bomb

Dropping nuclear bombs during a negotiation is not a criminal-like offense. In fact, it's a necessary and very powerful tool that you will need in a legitimate high-stakes negotiation to get what you want.

At the time you drop your nuclear bomb, getting what you want could be anything. You could be at a point in the negotiation where you want to change the atmosphere. You could be at the point in a negotiation where you want to regain your leverage. Or you might be at a point in the negotiation where you want to exert total control of the process.

That's exactly what US Soccer wanted to do on the first morning of the first day of CBA negotiations—to drop a nuclear bomb and wrestle immediate control of the negotiations before the negotiations even started!!

As I walked into the Latham & Watkins conference room in Midtown Manhattan on that bitter cold and gloomy morning of February 3, 2016, USSF's decades-long chief litigator and CBA negotiator Russ Sauer came out firing.

Rich, are you ready to agree that the USWNT does not have the right to strike or boycott the Olympics this year? Sauer blurted out.

That was the first bomb they dropped on us. Or so I thought. As the negotiation evolved, it occurred to me that this was in fact the Federation's second nuclear bomb. The deployment of spies from powerful consulting firm McKinsey & Company to infiltrate the players association in December 2015 was their first nuclear attack. More on that later.

At 4:45 p.m. that same day, after what had seemed to be an amicable all-day negotiation session, the second bomb came down.

"Rich, we just sued the players in federal court in Chicago seeking a declaratory judgment from the court proclaiming that the players do *not* have the right to strike or boycott the Olympics." Sauer said.

An unexpected nuclear blast that shook me and my colleagues to the core. I was numb, in a bit of shock, and a bit dazed and breathless.

As heavyweight fighter Henry Tillman, who beat Mike Tyson in the 1984 US Olympic boxing trials, and perennial world champion Sugar Ray Leonard each separately told me, it's the punch you don't see coming that can knock you out. Well, I wasn't knocked out, but close to it!

As a legal crisis management expert, I was now the client in crisis. I had just been sucker punched and I was reeling back on my heels desperately seeking the ropes of the ring to keep me from falling to the floor revealing absolute vulnerability. My mind was racing with a multitude of thoughts. *Stay calm ... don't show your fear to your teammates or the US Soccer representatives. Did the media know about the filing?* And my biggest fear of all was *what would the team think? Would they fire me and my team for being caught so unaware?*

My fears, thoughts, and existential uncertainty are the exact results dropping nuclear bombs are designed to elicit. Put your opponent on their heels. Cause them to rethink their strategies and objectives. Encourage them to seriously engage in the negotiation process with the sincere intent to reach an agreement.

Both of these US Soccer nuclear bombs accomplished at least three things for the federation.

First, they established immediately, even before we sat down at the negotiating table, that they were playing for "keeps"—and would *never* agree to equal pay.

Second, before the first negotiation session began, US Soccer forcefully grabbed the leverage right out of our hands as if to sing "How You Like Me Now?" by The Heavy, to our faces.

Third, the federation blindsided us with the totally unexpected federal lawsuit and threw us back on our heels. It was like Mike Tyson hitting you and knocking you silly with the first punch … *but this punch was delivered before the bell for the first round even sounded!*

Playing dirty or telegraphing desperation?

It meant Tyson, and in this instance, US Soccer, intended to kill you!

Tactically, for US Soccer, it was a brilliant strategy. They knew that despite my toughness, I had little CBA negotiating experience, and most importantly, that the players association had little to no money and would have a tough time financing the litigation to defend US Soccer's federal declaratory judgment lawsuit.

Yes, we were in trouble, and we now knew that the US Soccer Federation planned to pull out all stops and do whatever it takes to defeat the USWNT quest for equal pay … including, incredulously, *suing their own World Cup champion players in federal court* to strip them of their one and only legal economic weapon in their battle for equality … the right to strike.

Essentially, by dropping two nuclear bombs on us on the first day of negotiations, US Soccer made it crystal clear that they *never ever intended to and would never agree to equal pay!*

More importantly, their nuclear bombs had accomplished a few things for US Soccer.

First, they (a) snatched away any leverage I thought we, the players, had going into the CBA negotiations.

Second, they catapulted the USWNT players into a real-life federal court battle that at minimum would cost us $250,000 to defend. *The USWNTPA had no money and were broke, and US Soccer knew it.*

Third, the federation put me in a situation where I had to ensure that despite the lawsuit, the players maintained their *commitment* to equal pay while simultaneously refocusing the team from the quest for equal pay to defending the federal declaratory judgment claim in a mission-critical effort to retain our most powerful economic tool in our fight for equal pay, which was the right to strike and boycott the 2016 Olympics.

Clearly, nuclear bombs are essential and magnificently effective.

When to Drop the Nuclear Bombs

Nuclear bombs can be deployed when (a) you reach a point in the negotiation where you want to demonstrate to your constituents that you, in fact, do understand where you are in the negotiation, and that you are in control of the negotiation—even though you might not be.

Or, (b) you may be in a situation where, to no avail, you have used all of your weapons, and you've deployed all of your tactics and you're in a position where you just need to win and need a successful Hail Mary, and you are compelled to drop the ultimate nuclear bomb to do exactly that, to end the game of negotiation victorious.

Or, you can have a preordained plan that involves projecting ahead in the evolution of a negotiation and identifying potential situational triggers that may develop during the process that set the stage for the deployment of a nuclear bomb.

(With regard to the US women's soccer team's pursuit of equal pay, we had *four* nuclear bombs in our arsenal, each of which could be triggered at certain stages of the CBA negotiation process.)

But, if you need a new nuclear bomb, depending on the situation that you encounter during the negotiation, there are always ways to create one during the process.

Or, as evidenced by the situation with the notice letter (described below), you could be the unwitting victim or beneficiary of an unplanned creation of a nuclear bomb that could elevate or devastate you.

Setting the Stage

On November 30, 2015, in a meeting with US Soccer at their Chicago headquarters, we telegraphed to US Soccer the preliminary guidelines and objectives that the US women's soccer team planned to pursue in our upcoming CBA negotiations.

The pre-CBA negotiation meeting included player representatives Alex Morgan, Becky Sauerbrunn, Hope Solo, my co-counsel Arthur McAfee, and me.

For seventeen years, McAfee had served as senior counsel to the NFLPA's revolutionary executive director Gene Upshaw. McAfee guided the Players Association through numerous CBA battles with outcomes that garnered NFL Players an unprecedented, historic, and to this day unmatched 55 percent of the gross NFL revenues. US Soccer CEO Dan Flynn, general counsel Lisa Levine, and the US Soccer's general manager, Tom King, attended this pre-CBA negotiations planning session on behalf of US Soccer.

Even though the then-current MOU that governed the relationship between the players and the Federation didn't expire until December 31, 2016, I was invited by USSF president Sunil Gulati to be his guest in his luxury suite to watch the first game of the teams' post—World Cup championship Victory Tour in Pittsburgh in August 2015. I decided to take advantage of this opportunity to leverage Sunil into considering the commencement of negotiations for a new CBA as soon as possible before the end of 2015.

It was just me, Sunil, and his teenage son.

So, I decided to take this rare opportunity of private time with Sunil—whom I just met for the first time—to leverage the team's 2015 World Cup victory to get the USSF president and erstwhile *king* to agree to open negotiations for a new CBA, so that the USWNT could have a new deal done before the upcoming 2016 Olympic Games.

***

SINCE THE EXISTING MOU did not contain any provisions by which the Team and individual players could market themselves and the team for endorsement opportunities without the permission of US Soccer, it was imperative that a new CBA be operative as soon as possible to unilaterally enable the team and individual players to financially capitalize on their 2015 World Cup success prior to and after the 2016 Olympic Games without US Soccer's prevailing draconian restrictions that prohibited the players association and players from securing endorsement deals.

These sponsorship deals did not allow the players in any way to describe or identify themselves as members of the USWNT, or wear any colors that implied that they were on the team without the permission of US Soccer. These outrageous restrictions and the need to obtain US Soccer's approval scared away most potential corporate endorsements. In fact, these restrictions caused two major marketing agencies to refuse to represent the players association. Without being able to sell the players association with the USWNT, there was nothing to sell to a sponsor. The biggest restriction was US Soccer's right to approve or disapprove *all* endorsement deals.

***

SURPRISINGLY, SUNIL AGREED.

I was elated! Naively, I believed that by obtaining Sunil's agreement to start new CBA talks now, sixteen months prior to the expiration of the MOU and all of the existing player contracts, we had gained a huge advantage.

But, between August and November, Sunil dragged his feet and despite my repeated attempts to schedule initial CBA negotiation sessions, Sunil didn't agree to convene a preliminary CBA negotiation meeting with the team until late November 2015.

Gulati and US Soccer were already controlling the situation. Notwithstanding the four months it took to get the pre-CBA negotiations meeting with the US Soccer brass, we let them know that day that we were going to be very deliberate.

We let them know that we were going to be very serious in our pursuit to equalize compensation and playing conditions.

We let them know that we would insist on equalizing the so-called *lifestyle terms* with regard to housing, air transportation, and travel accommodations. The ongoing development of the US women's soccer team would be our primary and penultimate objective.

The US Soccer power triumvirate just looked across the table at us with—what I would later learn was their standard negotiation session countenance—non-emotive, blank stares and not much commentary or opinions about what we projected.

After about one hour and lots of talk by Solo, Morgan, and Sauerbrunn reciprocated with a lot of head notting from Flynn, Levine, and King, we left the meeting.

Notwithstanding the absence of emotion or reaction from Flynn, Levine, and King, we felt pretty good when the meeting ended. We wanted to be transparent, and we told US Soccer we were going to be clear about what our demands and proposals would be.

Before the meeting ended, we told Flynn that within four weeks we would provide US Soccer with a written collective bargaining agreement proposal by the beginning of January 2016.

McAfee, David Feher (Jeff Kessler's law partner), me, and the players' five-member CBA negotiating committee for the team, (Hope Solo, Alex Morgan, Megan Rapinoe, Becky Sauerbrunn, and Carli Lloyd) and eventually the entire USWNT, spent the next month developing our comprehensive CBA proposal.

The primary objective of the proposal was simple—*equal* pay, *equal* travel, *equal* hotel accommodations, *equal* per diem, and *equal* respect. In short, whatever US Soccer provided the US Men's National Soccer Team (USMNT), the USWNT wanted it and more if warranted.

In fact, the primary objective was across-the-board equality for the women. Essentially, the CBA proposal that the USWNT submitted to US Soccer demanded equal everything.

The perennial World Cup and Olympic champions wanted to be paid exactly what the substantially uncelebrated USMNT men were being paid.

The USWNT wanted equal accommodations in travel and hotel amenities and equal per diem—which is the money each player gets daily when you're on the road traveling to and from a game or while in residency to train (sometimes more than 250 days per year). Simply stated, the USWNT wanted to have *equal everything*.

Further, in at least one demand, the USWNT wanted more. The women wanted a creation of a robust, NFLPA-type group licensing plan. A group licensing plan would represent a financially game-changing component of the USWNT CBA proposal that, if agreed to between the USSF and USWNT in the CBA, would provide annual payments of at least $175,000 to each of the 24 USWNT players.

One of US Soccer's biggest financial mysteries was Soccer United Marketing, or as it was always referred to by its acronym SUM. SUM was the marketing agency to which US Soccer legally assigned all of its assets (name, image, likeness, logos, trademarks, colors, etc.) including, but not limited to the USMNT and USWNT, to sell into the television rights and corporate sponsorship marketplace. The objective was to generate huge revenues for the federation. Revenues raised by SUM were to be utilized to operate the federation and fund the USMNT and the USWNT.

By all accounts, SUM appeared to be doing its job.

However, how much revenue was raised by SUM through the sale of USSF's USWNT and USMNT, and how US Soccer deployed those revenues (e.g. how much was spent on the USMNT and USWNT respectively) were the questions of the day.

Additionally, the big three professional sports leagues, NFL, MLB, and NBA, each have group licensing programs negotiated with their respective players associations by which the players in each league are provided a pro rata share of a designated portion of annual corporate sponsorship revenues accrued by the league, and players are provided opportunities to participate in various promotional and advertising activations through the leagues and players associations and league group licensing plans.

For instance, the NFL/NFLPA CBA provided that in the first year of the CBA, the NFLPA's designated portion of NFL corporate sponsor revenue was $53 million. Accordingly, each of the approximately 2,000 active NFL players would receive their individual pro rata share of the $53 million dollars. Thus, each player would receive a check for $26,500 that year.

Moreover, the group licensing plan afforded players another potential opportunity to get paid from NFL corporate sponsors. Specifically, in collective bargaining, the league and the players associations determine how many players any one league sponsor may have access to for a promotional appearance or engagement. That tranche of players is called the "group." The league's corporate sponsors then have access to the group of players of its choosing for promotional purposes.

For instance, the NFL and the NFLPA determined that NFL sponsors could have access to up to a maximum of five players—the "group"—for any one marketing, advertising, or promotional opportunity. The sponsor company would then select which five NFL players it would like to participate in its promotion. The NFLPA would then notify those selected players that a sponsor chose them and if the player accepted the request, that player would then independently negotiate their own deal with the corporate sponsor.

Notably, each player in the NFL has up to two opportunities to reap financial benefits from the respective group licensing plan. Given the robustness of the NFL/NFLPA group licensing plan, McAfee and I created a GLP for the USWNT. In its 2015 annual financial summary, US Soccer reported receiving approximately $18,000,000 in marketing revenue from SUM.

Hence, mimicking the NFLPA's group licensing plan, we included the following in the equal pay CBA proposal. We proposed creation of a USWNT/USSF group licensing plan in which 25 percent or approximately $4.2 million dollars of the $18,000,000 SUM marketing proceeds from "selling" the USWNT and USMNT would be split pro rata amongst the twenty-four USWNT players. Each player would receive approximately $175,000. A USWNT "group" would be comprised of five players, each of whom would be available to USSF sponsors for promotional opportunities. Just like the working of the NFLPA/NFL group licensing plan, USSF sponsors would have access to group(s) of USWNT players and negotiate separate deals with each player that accepts the promotional opportunity. Accordingly, like the NFLPA's group licensing plan, the USWNT/USSF group licensing plan would provide USWNT players annual guaranteed pro rata payments and the "group" opportunity for additional endorsement deals with USSF sponsors.

Interestingly, notwithstanding the commitment to equal pay, in hindsight it's easy to recognize that some players were still a bit timid, cautious, and just generally uneasy about demanding equal pay from the master—US Soccer—after almost two decades of economic slavery. The uneasiness among some of the USWNT players was unsettling but understandable.

Demanding to be paid equally to the men's team was a bold, gutsy move. It required courage and some finesse in the initial presentation of the economic CBA demand for equal pay.

The demand for across-the-board equality was so out of the box for the USWNT that in hindsight it was, from our perspective, actually the USWNT's first nuclear bomb!

Memorably, during the final team teleconference to approve the content of the final CBA proposal, one marquee player plaintively wondered aloud, "Do you think we are asking for too much money?"

In the initial draft of our CBA proposal, we had demanded equal pay in the form of $290,000 per USWNT player per year, which equaled the compensation received by the men's team for playing an average of twenty games per year.

With her utterance of that question–which was not rhetorical—an audible weighty pause engulfed the call.

Sensing that maybe it was just uncomfortable optics, I suggested that instead of trumpeting the $290,000 figure, we merely insert the least amount of compensation the team could earn in equal pay if they were subject to the men's pay-to-play bonus-based compensation system and played twenty games per year at $5,000 per game which would be $100,000.

Essentially, in the men's pay-to-play compensation system, if the federation scheduled twenty games and they lost all twenty games, the men would be paid $5,000 per game or $100,000 per year, which was still $28,000 more than top twelve Tier 1 players on the USWNT were earning at that time. Remember the USWNT were playing upwards of thirty games each year, with an almost undefeated record!

The optic-driven minimum annual compensation of $150,000 was the equal pay verbiage inserted into our CBA proposal. The maximum annual compensation in the men's pay-to-play compensation system was $290,000 (if they won all their games). The men's minimum was $100,000. Given the USWNT's history of exemplary performance, a "champion" $2,500 per game premium was added to elevate their USWNT "equal" minimum to $150,000. After all, it was a negotiation, and we had leverage.

The USWNT's Unintended Nuclear Bomb

While we were finalizing the terms of our CBA proposal, Arthur McAfee, who was also an expert in labor law, told me that we had to file what is known as the National Labor Relations Act (NLRA) Section 8(d) letter with US Soccer.

Section 8(d) of the National Labor Relations Act (NLRA), which is the federal law that governs labor/management employee/employer collective bargaining negotiations in the United States, required that no later than sixty days prior to the date upon which an MOU/CBA modification or termination would be effective, the USWNT players association had to give US Soccer official notice that we intended to either modify or terminate the existing collective-bargaining agreement (e.g. the MOU) between US Soccer and the USWNT.

In short, our objective at the time was to negotiate a new CBA by March 1, 2016. Accordingly, per Section 8(d), if we planned to modify or terminate the terms of the MOU within sixty days after we submit our CBA proposal to USSF, we had a legal obligation to notify US Soccer of our objective.

All twenty-four USWNT players played on NWSL teams. Importantly, US Soccer paid the salaries of all twenty-four players to play in the NWSL. Notably, this economic arrangement required the USWNT players to have two jobs, one playing for the USWNT and another playing in the NWSL. US Soccer paying both salaries was codified as a term in the 2013 MOU.

It is important to note, that US Soccer had three tiers of compensation for USWNT players. Per the 2013 MOU, Tier 1, Tier 2 and Tier 3 USWNT Players earned $29,000, $21,000 and $7,000 respectively to play in the NWSL. Accordingly, although NWSL compensation was an additional source of income, it was clearly not a separate livable wage.

Also, in 2013, 2014, and 2015, given the fragility of the new NWSL, in order to guarantee that the USWNT players would actually get paid for playing in the NWSL, the Players did not enter into player contracts with the NWSL. Instead, in the 2013 MOU, US Soccer agreed to pay the USWNT players NWSL compensation.

Thus, in order for a USWNT player to get paid to play in the NWSL, they had to be on the USWNT.

In 2016, we faced the uncertainties with regard to the financial sustainability of the NWSL, coupled by the fact that during CBA negotiations, (a) US Soccer would NOT commit to continuing to pay the USWNT players NWSL compensation going forward in 2016 and beyond, (b) and or confirm US Soccer's continued financing of the fragile NWSL.

Given these facts, we (the USWNT) were compelled to negotiate the CBA accepting as reality that playing for the USWNT was indeed the players' only secure source of income—a reality that rendered impossible our ability to accept US Soccer's only "Pay-to-Play" counteroffer to our equal pay CBA proposal in May 2016.

At this point, I'd be remiss if I failed to acknowledge that with regard to the evolution of the NWSL, in early 2024–11 years after its inaugural 2013 season–two top NWSL players who most likely will be on the 2024 USWNT are reportedly earning in excess of $400,000 per year. However, the minimum NWSL salary remains at a non-livable wage of $36,400 per year.

Indeed, the reason the 2013 MOU was incomplete and devoid of potentially economically valuable provisions for players group licensing and individual player merchandising and marketing was that negotiating those financially valuable provisions would have taken too long. The inaugural 2013 NWSL season training camps opened on April 1, 2013, and USWNT players could not participate unless the CBA they were openly negotiating in December 2012 (when Hope Solo first called me) was complete and signed by the USWNT players. Since Hope convinced the players in January 2013 to hold out for higher salaries, by early March 2013, the CBA negotiations were nowhere near being complete.

So, trusting Gulati and Langel, the players agreed to defer negotiation of the group licensing plan and merchandising and player marketing provisions of the MOU until the final CBA was negotiated during the 2013 NWSL season.

It never happened.

When I took over the USWNTPA in January 2015, the horrendously incomplete MOU was still the document that governed the relationship between US Soccer and the players.

The failure to finalize the MOU into a valid, official collective bargaining agreement was just another element to the seemingly endless litany of disrespect the US Soccer Federation hoisted upon the powerhouse US Women's National Soccer Team over several decades.

Accordingly, pending the completion of CBA negotiations, US Soccer, and the USWNT through its players association, the US Women's National Team Players Association (USWNTPA), on March 19, 2013, agreed to enter into a memorandum of understanding or MOU which is essentially a term sheet or an agreement to agree. In essence, it is a form of collective bargaining agreement that governs the operational relationship between the parties until the final and formal collective bargaining agreement is finalized.

So, why did we want a new CBA by March 1, 2016?

Two reasons. First, the new NWSL season commenced with the opening of training camps on that date.

And second, US Soccer paid the twenty-four members of the US women's soccer team to play on the NWSL's teams. In 2013, those terms of payment would be included in the new collective bargaining agreement, which would be modified with a new compensation structure in the new agreement.

Thus, we had to give the 8(d) notice.

Going into the negotiations we were being very optimistic that we could come to a deal on a new CBA with US Soccer by March 1, 2016. I drafted the Section 8(d) notice letter and emailed it to USSF's general counsel, Lisa Levine, on Christmas Eve, December 24, 2015.

Little did I know at the time, this was going to be a turning point in the negotiations—even before the negotiations officially commenced.

To me, the letter was just an obligatory process communique. It was nothing other than providing US Soccer legally required notice of our intent to modify or terminate the MOU.

We submitted our CBA proposal to US Soccer on January 4, 2016. At that time, we had not received a response from US Soccer to the notice letter. To be honest, given the routine nature of the notice letter, I was not expecting a response.

However, between the day I submitted our CBA proposal to US Soccer in early January up to January 31, I did receive a couple of emails from Lisa Levine in which she encouraged me to talk to the USWNT's previous counsel, John Langel.

I ignored Levine's suggestion.

However, now I understand why Lisa was encouraging me to chat with Mr. Langel.

Apparently, as recounted by Sunil and John Langel, they had orally agreed between themselves on behalf of their respective clients that the no strike/no boycott provisions from the expired December 2012 CBA was—even though it's not written anywhere—incorporated by reference into the 2013 MOU, which did not expire until December 31, 2016. So, in January 2016, US Soccer essentially believed that the USWNT was still bound to the no strike/no boycott provision of the 2012 CBA.

As a result, since US Soccer interpreted the notice letter as a threat to strike or boycott the 2016 Olympic Games, Levine was directing my attention to Langel so he could school me with regards to the understanding or gentleman's agreement they had about the continued applicability of the 2012 CBA no strike/no boycott provision in the 2013 MOU.

I never contacted him.

In fact, it was Langel's deposition testimony in US Soccer's declaratory judgment case in which Langel testified that in fact, he and Gulati had discussed and agreed to retain that provision in the MOU.

The federal judge relied on Langel's deposition testimony to affirm US Soccer's position that the clause was incorporated by reference into the MOU—incredibly by verbal reference—because there was no written document—not even the MOU- that codified the no strike/no boycott restrictions.

Now I know why Lisa directed me to talk to Langel. She figured he'd inform me of his gentlemen's agreement with Gulati.

Unbeknownst to us, US Soccer had interpreted the notice letter as the drop of our first nuclear bomb. They assumed I knew about the applicability of the 2012 CBA's no strike/ no boycott provision and viewed the notice letter as a slap in the face notice of the team's intent to strike.

So, to head us off at the pass and assuming we planned to ignore the gentlemen's agreement, US Soccer sought the federal court declaratory judgment to strip the USWNT of its only economic tool in a CBA negotiation, the right to strike.

We wouldn't know it until February 3, 2016, as we walked into our first collective bargaining negotiation session, that US Soccer interpreted the notice letter as the dropping of a nuclear bomb.

Russ Sauer told us that the letter was actually a notice of the USWNT's plan to strike or boycott the Olympic Games if we did not agree to a CBA deal by March 1.

I was dumbfounded.

In truth, the USWNT *never* contemplated striking or boycotting the Olympic Games in 2016.

It was not on the USWNT's radar.

In fact, I never even thought about it, because I knew that there was *no way* that the women on the World Cup champion US Women's National Soccer Team were going to hurt the United States of America by striking or boycotting the 2016 Olympic Games in Rio.

No way.

It never crossed any of the players' minds.

It never crossed my mind.

It never crossed co-counsel McAfee's, Fehr's or Kessler's mind.

Striking or boycotting was never considered.

Therefore, we did not drop that nuclear bomb on US Soccer, but it didn't matter because that's how US Soccer saw it.

And US Soccer's interpretation of the notice letter which caused the federation to be the first to drop a nuclear bomb, set the stage for what would be a ferocious CBA battle.

US Soccer believed they had been sucker punched by the notice letter. Thus, they had to do something to regain leverage and control of the situation.

So, on February 3 as we walked into the negotiation session before we even sat down, Russ asked me out loud.

"Rich, are you ready to agree that you guys do not have the right to strike or boycott the Olympics this year?"

He was calling me out!!

But it didn't matter what I said. US Soccer had already decided six weeks before that my 8(d) notice letter was a nuclear bomb threat to strike or boycott that we dropped, and they were going to try to regain control of this negotiation process on the first day of negotiations by deploying their own nuclear arsenal.

And they did.

Remarkably, at the end of the first day of CBA negotiations, Russ Sauer, US Soccer's chief negotiator, announced that they had sued the USWNT players, the World Cup champions, in federal court in Chicago, asking a judge to issue a declaratory judgment stating that the

US Women's National Soccer Team did not have the right to strike or boycott the Olympic Games. Essentially, US Soccer totally blindsided us at the end of the first day of CBA negotiations and immediately regained control and leverage of that negotiation.

They had us on our heels rethinking our process. But the one thing US Soccer didn't have the USWNT rethinking was their objective.

The objective was equal pay, no matter what.

And the players were totally committed. In fact, even *more committed* after we informed them on the evening of February 3 that US Soccer had sued them. Yes, US Soccer had sued their most prized, valuable asset, their own World Cup champion players on the US Women's National Soccer Team.

In unison, the Players shouted over the teleconference line ... "Let's fight!"

US Soccer had sued the players to strip the World Cup and Olympic champions of the only economic tool employees have in labor versus management, collective bargaining negotiations—the right to strike and boycott your employer.

Perhaps ironically, the lawsuit just added fuel to the fire. The players' commitment to equal pay as the objective got stronger. Importantly, US Soccer's deployment and dropping of their first nuclear bomb on us failed to dislodge the top women of the US women's soccer team from their commitment to their primary objective, which was equal pay.

In fact, it emboldened the team.

Notably, we had our own set of nuclear bombs ready to deploy.

At this point, I guess it wouldn't hurt to take credit and label the 8(d) notice letter a nuclear bomb that we inadvertently deployed on US Soccer. We had four more nuclear devices in our arsenal beginning with our new CBA proposal, which among a host of novel economic demands, demanded equal pay.

Our CBA proposal demanded equal everything—whatever the USMNT had, and more.

The USWNT's 2016 CBA proposal demanded benefits that one would think these accomplished women would have already enjoyed. In addition to equal pay, the team demanded group licensing and marketing rights, separate standard player contracts for their two separate jobs providing professional services to their separate employers—the United States Soccer Federation and the National Women's Soccer League (NWSL), a comprehensive World Cup and Olympic team bonus compensation structure that mimics what the USMNT had, and health and safety protections that included not playing any games on artificial turf.

Remarkably, the US Soccer Federation had *never* provided the USWNT some basic benefits that employees in most industries enjoy, specifically 401(k) retirement plans and other related benefits and maternity and childcare coverage. Finally, given their status as professional athletes in a very physical sport in which players routinely experienced physical contact with the instrumentalities of their sport, the USWNT CBA proposal demanded the appointment of permanent team physicians and catastrophic injury insurance and a post-career player health care fund.

Nuclear Bomb #2

The second nuclear bomb that we were prepared to deploy was the historic action of filing USWNT player complaints with the United States Equal Employment Opportunity Commission (EEOC) alleging that US Soccer had violated the Equal Pay Act, and for twenty years had engaged in wage discrimination in violation of Title VII against the United States Women's National Soccer Team.

If we dropped this nuclear bomb, it would not only be historic, it would literally change the paradigm of the negotiation. Never before had professional athletes filed EEOC complaints against their current employer—thereby putting at risk their jobs, spots on the team, income, and careers—alleging wage discrimination and violation of the Equal Pay Act.

If and when we deployed this nuclear device, it would be an historic, gutsy move.

An EEOC filing by the high-profile, beloved worldwide World Cup and Olympic champion United States Women's National Soccer Team would change the landscape in the team's CBA negotiations and industrial environment for all women in the workplace, not only in sports, but in all industries.

Such courageous action would demonstrate to US Soccer and the world that if the United States Women's National Soccer Team can sue their current employer for wage discrimination and violation of the Equal Pay Act, then you too can empower yourself to confront your employer. And if, as a woman in the workforce, you think you have been discriminated against in terms of wages, additional compensation, and other benefits that the men who do the same job in the same work conditions currently enjoy, you too can file EEOC complaints against your employer to uncover the violations of law and ultimately remedy the economic disparities.

In short, EEOC complaints would be a globally empowering, nuclear bomb to drop.

And, at the appropriate time, we dropped that EEOC nuclear device on US Soccer.

***

MY STOMACH CHURNED for the entire six days before the call. It was scheduled for 3:00 p.m. Eastern on a Saturday afternoon in late March 2016.

As executive director of the players association, outside counsels, and general advisors, it is our duty to have tough conversations with our player clients. Communicating the gut-wrenching realities and acknowledging to clients and describing the painful decisions they'll have to make based on the law and the facts is commonplace for us. We lay out the pros and the cons, explain the decision that the players have to make, and clarify the potential consequences that will ensue after the decision is made. Then we step back and let the players make the decision.

But in this situation, it just felt a lot different.

These extraordinary women, these perennial world champions— Hope Solo, Alex Morgan, Becky Sauerbrunn, Megan Rapinoe, and Carli Lloyd, the player gut-wrenching presentatives of the USWNT—had placed their absolute trust in our hands. It was the classic David versus Goliath matchup. These powerful women had taken on an epic battle for equal pay against a formidable, well-financed juggernaut—the United

States Soccer Federation. The USSF is a soccer governing body second only in power to FIFA—an organization that literally controls the players' lives. On an peaceful early-spring Saturday afternoon, we were now going to ask them to do something disruptive, yet historic—something that had never been done before in professional sports, or for that matter, in any industry.

We were going to ask Solo, Morgan, Rapinoe, Sauerbrunn, and Lloyd to sue their current employer, the United States Soccer Federation, and accuse the organization that essentially had total control of their lives of violating the Equal Pay Act and wage discrimination under Title VII.

The call started on time. We laid out the history of our three months of CBA negotiations with US Soccer. We explained how David Feher, Rapinoe, Art McAfee, and I had attended all of our negotiation sessions and come to the conclusion that absent the deployment of a nuclear option, US Soccer was *never* going to budge or even consider equal pay. Even the decorated sports lawyer Jeff Kessler, who for decades led players in the NFL and the NBA Players Associations to billion-dollar payday CBAs, agreed with our conclusions.

As a result, we had to take drastic action.

So, we discussed with the players a filing of a complaint(s) with the Equal Employment Opportunity Commission (EEOC) alleging that the United States Soccer Federation had violated the Equal Pay Act and Title VII by engaging in wage discrimination against the USWNT for the past twenty years.

We explained to the players that this had never been done before, and that this was historical. Never before have professional athletes sued their current employer for wage discrimination. Never before had professional women in any industry sued their current employer for violation of the Equal Pay Act.

Until now.

I took a deep breath and said, "To take this action, to make this decision would be game-changing—not only for you women on the United States Women's National Soccer Team, but it would be a game-changer for women in every industry and every woman in a workforce on the face of the earth. You would be pioneers and role models to women in the workforce who suffer from not being paid equally to their male counterparts. You would be providing the roadmap for women to follow to get equal pay."

We also explained that filing the complaint would be courageous and dangerous, but it would also be groundbreaking. In order to effect real change, not only in the collective bargaining negotiation but real change in the work world for women, this action *had* to be taken.

We paused for a few seconds to let it all sink in, and then we explained that we needed at least two of the players to sign the complaints. Incredibly, before we could say another word, all five players said in unison, "We'll all sign, Rich, We'll all sign, Rich … all of us!

I felt a warm flush over my entire body. I knew that the game had just changed.

But I also knew that the hard part had really just begun.

And for me, as a Black lawyer, I knew that for the players' historic EEOC claims to be viewed as credible and meritorious, in order for these women to be taken seriously, given modern-day realities, I had to fade into the background.

For any employee, filing an EEOC complaint and suing their current employer for violation of the Equal Pay Act and Title VII is a huge, courageous undertaking. Needless to say, filing EEOC complaints and suing the employer—the United States Soccer Federation—alleging Title VII wage discrimination and violation of Equal Pay Act would be a breathtaking, brave, historic step, not only in professional sports but in the general, industrial, and professional workplace for women all over the world.

These five brave women on the United States women's national soccer team dropped the nuclear bomb.

They jeopardized their careers.

They jeopardized their incomes.

They jeopardized their spots on future World Cup and Olympic teams.

And they ran the risk of being banished for life from the sport that they loved. But they did it anyway, they did it proudly, and they did it without any reservation.

So, when they filed their complaints, I knew that I had a huge responsibility to make sure that these women would be taken seriously.

Accordingly, Jeff Kessler and I arranged for the players to announce the historic filing of their EEOC complaints on the first 7:00 to 7:20 a.m. segment of NBC's *Today* show. Matt Lauer would do the questioning. My preference was to give the "scoop" to and make the announcement on *Good Morning America* with Robin Roberts who is not only a friend, but a longtime supporter of equality for women in professional sports. (Robin would have invested in the ABL in 1996 but couldn't due to ESPN's conflict of interest.)

Additionally, I also didn't trust Matt Lauer with this decidedly female-empowering story, and worried he'd find a reason to attack Hope Solo during the segment—which despite his producer's promise would not happen, did happen at the end of the segment when Lauer snuck in a last-minute stab at Hope's then fear of the Zika virus spreading in Brazil, the site of that summer's Olympic Games. We knew that this big-time, prime-time public announcement was the only way to communicate to the world the magnitude of the action Solo, Morgan, Sauerbrunn, Rapinoe, and Lloyd were taking.

Deep down inside I also knew that, notwithstanding that it was 2016, there was no way that these high-profile white women who were suing their high-profile white employer alleging discrimination of any kind would be taken seriously if they were represented by a Black lawyer.

Their claims would be cast aside as ludicrous—a publicity stunt. And I knew it. Art McAfee, my Black co-counsel and seasoned NFLPA/NFL CBA negotiator, agreed with my assessment.

This was one of the reasons I hired Kessler in November 2015 to serve as our outside counsel.

When it was abundantly clear that we would in fact seek equal pay in the upcoming January 2016 CBA negotiations, I knew the risk of these fearless women not being taken seriously because of the hue of their legal counsel was real.

I had known Kessler for twenty years. In 1997, when I was general counsel for the American Basketball League (ABL)—the premier women's professional basketball league and catalyst for the NBA's begrudging creation of the WNBA—I hired Kessler to lead the ABL's prospective pursuit of an antitrust lawsuit against the NBA.

In November 2015, I called Kessler in Japan. I explained the team's mission. Without hesitation, he joined our legal team.

I emailed the team to announce the new addition. Megan Rapinoe's—who in 2016 had not yet risen to her present level of fame and notoriety—response was memorable and expected:

"We are in the big-time now!"

I was not naïve.

In order for me to survive as a Black lawyer in this high-stakes, high-profile, very public game—I knew that the optics had to depict that the all-powerful, successful white sports lawyer was *really* in charge of this incredibly high-stakes, groundbreaking game.

In preparation for going on primetime, at 5:30 a.m., the five history-making USWNT players in an Orlando pre-Olympic training camp hotel sleepily found their way from their respective rooms to the ballroom set for pre-show make-up sessions and coffee. Accordingly, twenty minutes before air-time on the *Today* show remote set in a hotel, I pulled Kessler aside and told him that he would sit on the live set with the players to announce the filing of these EEOC claims. Not me.

Jeff couldn't understand.

He said, "Rich, why don't you do it? You've been the leader, this was your idea, so you should do it, you should sit on the set with the players as they announce this to the world."

I said, "No Jeff, you do it. Trust me, it'll be better that way".

And so it was. Alex Morgan, Becky Sauerbrunn, Megan Rapinoe, Carli Lloyd, Hope Solo, and Tom Brady's famous sports lawyer Jeff Kessler announced to the world on the *Today* show on March 30, 2016, that history had been made and that these five women had filed complaints with the EEOC alleging that US Soccer had violated the Equal Pay Act and Title VII, and had engaged in wage discrimination against the World Cup and Olympic champion United States Women's National Soccer Team.

Art and I stood proudly off to the side of the *Today* show set as the segment aired.

Nuclear Bomb #3 — EEOC Filing Media Blitz

Another nuclear bomb that would serve to promote the EEOC filings would be deployed after we filed the EEOC complaints.

The *Today* show announcement would be followed by a bold strategic seven-week media onslaught and presence where US Soccer was viscerally engaged and excoriated by the team in all forms of world media, by exposing the federation's considerable ugly warts and penchant for the inequality and metaphoric decades-long inequitable behavior.

The panorama was ugly, especially when juxtaposed against the undeniable historical incidences of disparate treatment to which these courageous women were subjected, despite their huge successes and ironic status as the biggest revenue-generating engine of the federation.

During the two months of unrelenting, penetrating onslaught of media in which US Soccer was hard-pressed to defend its decades of wage discrimination, the world learned that the men's team was paid *75 percent more than the US Women's National Soccer Team*, who were perennial, Olympic champions and three-time World Cup champions—as delineated in the players' EEOC complaints. The women were being paid slave wages and shamefully treated like indentured servants by the United States Soccer Federation.

We vowed to expose those inequalities in the media for as long as it took for the world to understand what these women had endured for two decades.

Unforgiving, egregious, and unimaginable disparate treatment.

Just plain despicable.

We were confident that the media-blitz nuclear bomb, and the constant exposure of the inequities and inequalities suffered by these courageous USWNT women would be recognized by all across the world. In turn, the world would put intolerable pressure on the United States Soccer Federation by paying huge attention to the horrible treatment of the most prized and successful asset, which is the US Women's National Soccer Team.

True to form, the Democratic women in the United States Senate led by the late Senator Dianne Feinstein took notice, grabbed the lapels of their male Democratic Senate colleagues, and answered the team's call.

A quick backstory about Senator Feinstein. It had been almost twenty-five years since I last had contact with her. During my days working in politics and city government in the City and County of San Francisco in the mid- to late 1980s, I had the honor and privilege of working with Senator Feinstein when she was mayor of San Francisco. I was a legislative aide to supervisor Willie B. Kennedy, at the time the widow of Joseph Kennedy, the first Black Superior Court Judge in San Francisco, who went to San Francisco State University in her late forties and graduated at the age of fifty magna cum laude with a degree in broadcast journalism. Wille B, as we all affectionally called her, had a calling for public service.

In 1982, Mayor Feinstein appointed her to the San Francisco Board of Supervisors to fill an unexpired term. Kennedy ran for reelection in 1984 and was elected in her own right. However, she did not want to be known as a Feinstein clone, and wanted to build her own political persona in San Francisco. To my great fortune, she hired me to help her achieve that objective. Again, I gravitated toward a very strong woman and signed on to assist her evolution in the raucous world of city politics in San Francisco.

Feinstein was a bit more conservative than Supervisor Kennedy, but generally, their legislative agendas were symbiotic. Kennedy had a keen interest in South Africa, the political imprisonment of Nelson Mandela, and that country's fight to end apartheid. Naturally, she came up with the idea of introducing a South African divestment Ordinance that would prohibit the City and County of San Francisco from doing business with any company doing business in South Africa. "Doing business" had a broad definition—so broad that it included companies that were headquartered in San Francisco. Essentially, if you were headquartered in San Francisco and did business in South Africa and paid taxes to the city, that constituted "doing business" and you were no longer welcomed in the city unless you divested whatever business activities you conducted in South Africa.

Whoa!!

Chevron and the Bank of America were both headquartered in San Francisco. Both companies had significant holdings and operating entities in South Africa. So, if they did not divest those holdings and business units, they had to leave San Francisco. No exceptions!

That was the edict from supervisor Kennedy. She was tough and told the world, including her benefactor Mayor Feinstein, that she would *not* relent. Mayor Feinstein, also a tough, take-no-prisoners woman, vowed that she'd find a solution that would allow the companies to stay, and for supervisor Kennedy to get her historic South African divestment ordinance on the books.

Ultimately, Feinstein's Chief of Staff Jim Lazarus and I painstakingly negotiated what's known as a "sunset provision" to cover the Bank of America and Chevron. Specifically, the ordinance was amended to include a provision that gave each company five years to wind down their respective business dealings in South Africa and not enter any new South African engagements. Both companies agreed to the compromise, and Mayor Feinstein signed the United States's first municipal South African divestment ordinance into law.

Two strong courageous women found common ground and were the genesis of laws that slowly but surely deprived the apartheid regime precious revenues from US-based companies.

That was in 1987.

Feinstein and Kennedy were my heroes. I stayed in touch with Dianne until she was elected to the US Senate in 1993. In fact, she offered me the job as her Northern California field representative, but I wanted to practice law and took a job in the San Francisco City Attorney's Office.

So, in April 2016 when I picked up the phone and called Senator Feinstein's office to ask for her help in this battle with US Soccer for equal pay, it had been twenty-three years since we connected and I wasn't even sure she'd remember me. I chatted briefly with Jennifer Duck, Feinstein's chief of staff, and told her what I wanted and waited for a call back. The very next morning, Jennifer called me, told me that Senator Feinstein indeed remembered me, and asked me to come to DC as soon as I could to meet and talk about how the Senator could help.

Elated, I flew there almost immediately. Unbeknownst to me, our nuclear bomb media blitz had struck a sensitive cord in the House of Representatives, many of whom were outraged that the USWNT was being paid slave wages by US Soccer. Unsolicited by me, almost two hundred members of Congress signed a letter sent to the US Soccer Federation urging the federation to do the right thing and pay the USWNT equally. Likewise, twenty-five US senators joined them. Senator Feinstein took it a step further and convened a meeting with the top brass of US Soccer—CEO Dan Flynn and General Counsel Lisa Levine—to put some equal pay heat on them.

All we really needed was a hearing either in the US Senate Commerce Committee or the Judiciary Committee to put Sunil Gulati and Dan Flynn and other US Soccer officials on the hot seat and air out US Soccer's dirty laundry with regard to why they don't provide equal pay. But, the Republicans controlled the Senate and in order to get a hearing, at least one Republican senator needed to call for one.

Not one Republican stepped forward to call a hearing. We almost convinced then Republican freshman Senator Shelley Capito from West Virginia to do it, but ultimately, she succumbed to the weight of her lack of seniority and leverage with her senior Republican Senate colleagues who opposed a hearing.

We were close, but no cigar.

Nuclear Bomb #4

A fourth weapon in our nuclear arsenal was the ubiquitous, world-renowned, influential news magazine, CBS's *60 Minutes*.

Make no mistake, if truth is to be found, *60 Minutes* will find it and deliver it to you every Sunday evening at 7:00 p.m.

No one in the crosshairs of a major public controversy that involves alleged malfeasance, crimes, or other types of wrongdoing wants to be the target of a *60 Minutes* investigation. Indeed, everyone knows that when *60 Minutes* comes calling and gets a chance to look under your tent, if anything bad is happening inside, *60 Minutes* is going to uncover it. They are going to give one an opportunity to address and defend what *60 Minutes* has discovered, and expose it for the entire world to see.

Around early August 2016, *60 Minutes* came calling at the Chicago headquarters of the United States Soccer Federation to talk to President

Sunil Gulati and other US Soccer executives about USWNT demands for equal pay and the federation's history of unfair treatment of the World Cup champions. The US Soccer Federation's sweat glands jacked-up into overdrive!

To say that *60 Minutes* is selective in the investigations they decide to pursue would be a gross understatement. CBS budgets hundreds of thousands of dollars and spends a minimum of four months vigorously investigating topical issues that culminate in a 13-minute, 13-second long powerful television investigative, hard to the bone report. Their investigations are thoughtful, provocative, gut-wrenching, revealing, and unforgiving fact-finding missions.

Well, when 60 Minutes knocked on the doors of the United States Soccer Federation to talk to them about the USWNT's EEOC allegations of wage discrimination and violations of Title VII and the Equal Pay Act, figuratively, US Soccer did *not* answer the door.

So, you might ask, how did we get *60 Minutes*?

How did we get the great award-winning, blockbuster journalist Norah O'Donnell, *60 Minutes,* and CBS News to investigate US Soccer and our quest for equal pay?

In April 2016, one of many substantive results of Nuclear Bomb #3, specifically, the seven-week media blitz after filing of the EEOC Complaints against US Soccer, was the fact that CBS News and *The Atlantic* magazine took note of the courageous action of the five women. CBS News' Norah O'Donnell—a longtime fan of women's soccer and admirer of Hope Solo—took note that Solo had basically led these women to pursue equal pay.

As a result, Hope and I were invited to the 2016 White House Correspondents Dinner (WHCD) as guests of CBS News and *The Atlantic*. It would be President Obama's last White House Correspondents Dinner. Hope and I were exuberant about the invitation to attend this historic event.

The night before the WHCD dinner, David Bradley, the CEO of *The Atlantic,* hosted a one-hundred-person sit-down invitation-only dinner at his home in Washington, DC. Hope and I were invitees.

At the reception before the dinner, I had the good fortune of meeting Norah O'Donnell.

Norah and I hit it off right away. Unlike many celebrity journalists, Norah was easy to talk to, very humble, whip-smart, gracious, and a rabid sports enthusiast. Interestingly, Norah had been a high school track and field athlete. In fact, she shared with me that in high school in Houston, Texas, she ran the 400 meters and posted a pretty respectable time, 58 seconds, as a senior. Given that I was a former a member of the United States Track & Field team in the early 1980s, Norah and I had a lot to talk about.

Naturally, I saw this as an opportunity to sell Norah on the Hope Solo-led USWNT quest for equal pay and US Soccer's sordid history of economic and workplace gender discrimination and oppression against the USWNT as a great story for *60 Minutes* to investigate.

As the saying goes in sports, I grabbed the baton and I ran with it.

I walked Norah through the whole history of the US women's soccer team and their mistreatment by US Soccer dating back to that celebrated 1999 World Cup championship game against China.

I told Norah about how Hope Solo had called me in December 2012, extremely frustrated and totally fed up with US Soccer's refusal to pay them adequate compensation, and fed up with the comprehensive disrespect that for decades these strong women, and perennial World Cup and Olympic champions had endured from US Soccer.

I explained to Norah, when the team finally engaged me in January 2015, the fight for equal pay and all that comes with equality began.

And I told Norah it culminated with the filing of the historic EEOC complaints.

After about an hour of a seemingly nonstop discussion, Norah said to me, "Rich, I think this is a *60 Minutes* story." To which I replied, "That's what I was hoping you'd say!"

Norah couldn't wait to meet Hope.

"Rich, I'm going pass this by my producers, I'm going run it up to *60 Minutes* flag pole, and if they are interested, I'll call you and let you know. And it won't take long, I'll be calling you with a thumbs up or thumbs down within a week, and if it's a go here's what's going to happen," Norah continued.

"Within a week of the go, I'm going to call you with my top producer on the call and we are going to grill you hard for up to ninety minutes about everything you just told me."

"We're going to test your resolve, we're going to test the depths of your knowledge of the history of the USWNT collective bargaining efforts with US Soccer. We're going to test your capacity to pursue what you're pursuing on behalf of this team. Basically, my producer needs to walk away from our discussion feeling that this is more than just a bunch of puff and fluff and BS, that it's real, and that whatever the result, the efforts and pursuit of the team for equal pay will have a game-changing effect in the battle for equality—we will take on the story."

Norah's delivery was intense and challenging. I remember having a tightness in the pit of my stomach. I had no doubt that after my grilling, they'd pursue the investigation.

This was the real deal. This was *60 Minutes*.

This was no BS.

This was really going to happen.

True to form, about one week later, unannounced at 10:00 a.m. on a Tuesday, I got the call from Norah and her top producer, Keith Sharman. As promised, for the next ninety minutes they put me through a grueling, but manageable, deep dive into everything I had told Norah about the history of the US women's soccer team and their abuse at the hands of US Soccer.

At the end of the call, they just thanked me and hung up.

Two days later, Norah called me and said *60 Minutes* was in.

Norah would lead a *60 Minutes* investigation on the US Women's National Soccer Team's battle with the US Soccer Federation for equal pay.

Needless to say, I was exhilarated. I immediately called Hope and told her. She was over the moon!.

Having the opportunity to expose the gender-discriminating male executives that run US Soccer, and who abuse the women on the US soccer team, on a national platform like *60 Minutes* was going to be a serious game-changer, one way or the other.

The whole world was going to see exactly what the federation did not want exposed.

One way or the other you might ask?

Yes.

One by-product of the *60 Minutes* expose could be an immediate *mea culpa* from US Soccer in the form of an immediate agreement that yes, the federation has discriminated against these women and yes, US Soccer will pay them equally beginning immediately.

On the other end of the spectrum, another response from US Soccer could be the immediate firing of the players on the current USWNT, terminating their contracts and the termination of the CBA negotiations.

Indeed, the mere invocation of a *60 Minutes* investigation of US Soccer and its relationship with the USWNT would, in any event, be a game-changer.

Well, incredibly, but in hindsight not surprisingly, Gulati refused to cooperate with the *60 Minutes* investigation. Incredibly, no one from US Soccer talked to *60 Minutes* and the federation did not participate in the report.

Notwithstanding the federation's snub of Norah O'Donnell and *60 Minutes*, on November 20, 2016, with millions and millions of lead-in viewers who had just watched an overtime NFL game, and stacked in the middle of three stories, preceded by a profile of music phenom Bruno Mars, *60 Minutes* aired *The Match of Their Lives*, chronicling in painstaking detail the USWNT's hot battle for equal pay.

It was a bombshell.

Additional weeks of negative media scrutiny for US Soccer followed the *60 Minutes* broadcast.

The news media circuit was dissecting the report like a prosecutor grills a defendant on the witness stand.

The *60 Minutes* report and the early December 2016 EEOC Investigation Status Report—delivered by the EEOC to the players and US Soccer representatives in separate same-day telephone calls—catapulted the team into the equal pay red zone. Succinctly stated, the 2016 EEOC report detailed how the EEOC communicated (in separate calls) to both US Soccer and the players that they were leaning towards concluding that US Soccer had violated the equal pay act.

Experiencing the players glow in the "red zone" and feeling the painful singe of the "blue flame" signaling their imminent demise in the flames of equal pay, US Soccer decided it was time to do whatever they had to do to extinguish the burn.

7

Tactic III: Guts

BRAVADO? COURAGE? DETERMINATION? ... GUTS!

Webster's Dictionary defines it as having courage and determination.

Well, it certainly required courage and indefatigable determination for the twenty-four women on the 2015 World Cup champion roster to throw down the proverbial gauntlet and demand equal pay from the United States Soccer Federation (USSF).

After filing the historic, unprecedented EEOC complaints, it took big USWNT courage to create and execute a massive seven week, in-your-face, international media campaign to make the world aware of the abject wage discrimination they faced despite being perennial Olympic and World Cup champions.

It required even more courage and determination to persist and navigate US Soccer's eleven-month, non-stop nuclear bomb campaign during which the federation sued the players in federal court on the first day of equal pay collective bargaining agreement (CBA) negotiations in February 2016—to strip the players of their right to strike or boycott; continuously engaged in unfair labor practices; stonewalled CBA negotiations for several months while refusing to provide a response to the players' CBA negotiable demand for equal pay; infiltrated the players association with moles from the federation's management consultant— the renowned McKinsey & Company—ostensibly to, under the guise of helping the Players Association, dilute the influence of the players association leadership with the hope of eventually, at the very least, dissuading the players from their pursuit of equal pay.

So yes, it took big-time guts to fight US Soccer.

And yes, it took an infinite amount of courage to persist in the equal pay fight.

In the end, because of their persistence and never-say-die attitude, US Soccer had to pull out their biggest nuclear weapon to rearrange the USWNT's attitude ... to soften their iron-willed resolve, and kick them full throttle in a vulnerable spot where existential pain could not be ignored ... in the form of the unspoken, yet very real prospect of suffering the same fate as Hope Solo—that being termination of their jobs, income, and spots on the US national team if they did not give up their equal pay fight.

The USWNT players' choice was simple: either abandon the fight for equal pay or persist and risk the experience of professional and career suicide.

Despite their outsized courage and determination, these women were human. They carried the ball for equal pay to the red zone only to be defeated by the innate human condition, the human existence which required sustenance and income to literally survive.

But in the wake of their survival battle, they left an impressive trail and real blueprint for the quest and path that women coming after them can follow in their own pursuit of equal pay.

***

Of course, it took time to establish guts. It took time for the team to convince themselves that they had the courage, determination, strength, leverage, resolve, commitment and the power to get equal pay.

But once the USWNT players decided that they, in fact, had the guts, and were ready to move forward to blaze the trail to achieve their goal of equality, they moved with full force.

8

Tactic IV: Commitment

FIRM COMMITMENT.

That's what it's going to take for women in sports if they are ever going to be paid equally.

Firm resolve, steadfastness, will, obligation, vow … the same kind of *championship resolve to win* that top-tier athletes instinctively possess.

That same championship mentality that drives champions to commit to do whatever it takes to win championships.

That same resolve and drive that propels a Tiger Woods, Edwin Moses, Michael Jordan, Kobe Bryant, Jackie Joyner-Kersee, Marion Jones, Hope Solo, Brittney Griner, to relentlessly pursue success. It's the same drive and *commitment* that is required to attain equal pay.

Interestingly, the entire premise of commitment has a lot of similarities between the professional female basketball players of the ABL and the World Cup and Olympic champion members of the 2016 USWNT.

Just like in 2016 with Gulati's control of the Olympic dreams of players pushing for equal pay on the US Women's National Soccer Team, twenty years earlier in 1996, David Stern knew that he controlled the destiny and futures and 1996 Olympic dreams of each of the twelve members of the United States women's basketball team.

Just as Gulati knew, if any member of the US Women's National Soccer Team did anything that he decided could hurt US Soccer, he could kick that player off the team. Stern knew he had the same leverage, power, and authority with regard to the US women's basketball team.

He knew it, and every player on the team knew it.

For the ABL, since the prevailing economics of men's professional basketball internationally and in the NBA were not comparable, the ABL players' objective was equity—fairness, with regard to their compensation and work conditions.

For the US Women's National Soccer Team, despite US Soccer's pronouncements that the USMNT generated more revenue than the USWNT, according to US Soccer's 2014-15 financial statements, and projecting ahead in the federation's financial pro formas to 2019, the USWNT generated substantially *more revenue* that the US Men's National Soccer Team. Accordingly, the economics of men's and women's professional soccer in the USA were more than comparable. In fact, with the proof in US Soccer's own financials, the economic prowess of USWNT far exceeded that of the US men's team. As accurately proclaimed by the federation, the USWNT is the economic engine of the USSF.

Thus, *equality* was the USWNT's objective.

Equal pay for doing the same job as the US Men's National Soccer Team under the same work conditions.

That's what USWNT players wanted.

But for the ABL players, and players on the United States Women's National Soccer Team, if the objective was to be obtained, *total commitment* to the objective was required.

In both situations, these skilled, smart, strong, exceedingly confident, and courageous women blazed a Lewis and Clark–type trail pursuing equity (ABL) and equality (USWNT). What they did had never been done before. Thus, there was no path to follow.

Though, as a result of the intervention of life's realities—e.g. the need for income and an opportunity to continue to earn a living doing what they loved to do—the ABL players and the USWNT did not fully achieve their respective objectives.

Unfortunately, "life's circumstances" forced them to fall short on their commitment to their respective objectives. The ABL players did not achieve "equity" and the USWNT did not get "equal" pay.

But they did leave a blueprint for future women in the workforce seeking equal or equitable compensation to adopt. At the very least, the blueprint and carved-out trail, provides women that come after them the ingredients required and well-worn, dog-eared map to follow to get to the "promised land."

Succinctly stated, all of these women risked their careers, their jobs, their incomes, their livelihoods, and their personal and professional reputations to pursue an objective which was equity in the ABL and equality for the US national women's soccer team. They sustained their respective commitments to their respective objectives as long as they were able to. Ultimately, for a few of the ABL players and all of the USWNT (except Hope Solo), commitment was overpowered by intimidation and threat of job loss—all real human conditions—shamelessly leveraged by powerful men in their respective governing positions in the NBA and the United States Soccer Federation.

To be clear, this is *not* a negative result.

Because, as a result of the ABL and USWNT's respective journeys, women now know upfront, that it will take *total commitment* to the objectives to scale and blast through the walls erected to keep them from their goals to get to the end zone and score the equity or equal pay touchdown.

That's what they are going to have to do.

Maintain the commitment.

From Commitment to Collapse

It all came crumbling down on September 1, 2016.

Carli Lloyd called me to tell me that a top player stood up in a team meeting to proclaim that "Rich is stealing our money!"

With the utterance of that false statement, I knew my days as executive director of the Players Association were numbered. I knew that I might not survive until the *60 Minutes* piece aired.

I knew that since Hope was fired one week earlier on August 24, ostensibly for having publicly branded their Swedish national team opponents as "cowards" after the Swedes eliminated the World Cup champion USWNT in the quarterfinals of the Olympics, that US Soccer had stripped my strength from the team.

I knew that front and center US Soccer was coming after me ... and they weren't going to let up until I was gone.

McKinsey & Company was US Soccer's longtime management consulting firm. So, when, in addition to the false proclamation about me, Becca Roux, an analyst and lawyer from McKinsey & Company, arrived back on the scene with certain players—I knew the federation was about to apply the full-court press on the players, who would then be encouraged to fire me.

I was now facing the classic three-pronged elimination of a "labor leader" strategy being deployed by the USSF and executed by McKinsey.

First prong: *Accuse the head of the union of financial mismanagement, preferably, theft of funds or embezzlement. Hence, the "Rich is stealing our money" exhortation.*

Second prong: *Accuse the union head of negotiating terms in a prospective new CBA that have not been approved by the union membership, in this case, the USWNT.*

If the first two prongs fail or are alternately successful, *accuse the executive director (me) of providing improper advice with regard to members' possible outcomes if there is no new CBA prior to the expiration of the existing CBA, in this case, the MOU that was set to expire on December 31, 2016.*

In order to provide the players an opportunity to openly question me and McAfee on any and all subjects including the finances of the Players Association, I called an all-hands-on-deck meeting to be held in Atlanta on Saturday, September 18 to address the first two prongs flung at me in tandem in early September by a few players.

Two days prior to the meeting, I forwarded each team member the year-to-date financials as produced by the USWNTPA accountant, and the twenty-one voluminous emails I had sent to each team member between August 30, 2015, to that present day in September 2016 that chronicled every tactic pursued and every term negotiated. All five CBA negotiation sessions convened in 2016, and every facet of information they needed to stay up to date and informed with the status and progress of CBA negotiations were memorialized in those emails.

Art McAfee and I convened the meeting. It started at about 8:00 a.m. and concluded just after noon. During the meeting,

I painstakingly reviewed each of the aforementioned twenty-one emails that chronicled CBA negotiations, took and answered scrupulous questions about revenues and expenditures down to the penny, and answered questions about what will happen if we got to December 31 and did not have deal.

In short, Art and I faced the music—head-on. We were quite proud of our performance.

Frankly, I was hurt by the accusations that I was stealing their money. When I assumed leadership of the USWNTPA, because the organization was for all intents and purposes, broke, I reduced my already reduced fee of $10,000 per month to $6,000 per month. Given the time and commitment required to operate a players association—alone—$6,000 per month was a mere pittance ... $20,000 per month was the market rate for such services. Exemplifying his commitment to the equal pay objective, because of the players association's lack of funds, McAfee provided his legal services for free for almost one year.

But we survived that grilling.

Now, going into October 2016 and looking to our next October 26 CBA negotiation session, I knew I'd be pressed hard by the team about what will happen if by December 31 we did not have a deal.

Would they all lose their jobs when the MOU/CBA and their contracts expired on December 31?

The answer: Maybe. Indeed, the not-so rhetorical question that hung over their heads was with regard to total commitment and unanimity. Did they still have it? Given the pressure US Soccer and McKinsey were about to apply to dislodge their commitment to equal pay, could the team sustain their 100 percent commitment to equal pay?

9

Tactic V: Execution

AS NOTED EARLIER, historically, progress to equal pay has been incremental. Notably, though not totally satisfying, incremental progress was acceptable if continuing to push forward to eventual equality in pay remained the ultimate objective.

Importantly, the USWNT determined that "incremental," or anything less than equal pay was not acceptable. Accordingly, the team *committed* to pursue a plan to get equal pay. Anything less than 100 percent equal pay was unacceptable. Now, the challenge for the USWNT was *"execution"* and realization of that *"commitment."*

As a result, in this rare tactical scenario in which an "all or nothing" 100 percent result is required in order to execute the equal pay commitment, commitment and execution necessarily evolve as a "one in the same" combined tactic.

Of the five required tactics in the schematic road to equal pay, *execution* is the only one that touches each of the other four required methodical steps. The team had to execute and exploit leverage. The team had to execute and timely deploy their nuclear bombs. The team had to execute and throughout the equal pay journey execute and leverage their guts. The team had to execute and activate their "execution" of the equal pay plan. The team had to execute and stay true to their

100 percent commitment to secure equal pay. And ironically, when "execution" is necessarily combined with "commitment"—100 percent commitment is the tactic which the USWNT failed to fully execute and satisfy.

Webster's Dictionary defines *execution* as, "the ability to carry out fully; to accomplish; to put into effect; to do what is required."

Now, the sports definition of *execution* is "to properly perform the fundamental moves or the mechanics of your objective."

If one were to define the USWNT's performance with regard to pursuing equal pay, one would conclude that by application of the generic definition of "execution," in this case, "to carry out fully and to accomplish," the team failed.

Why?

Well, although the USWNT got to the last steps of equal pay, the team failed to execute their 100 percent commitment to do whatever was required to achieve equal pay. The USWNT got to the red zone—a descriptor used prominently in American football to telegraph imminent success—and had the ability to thwart US Soccer's considerable defensive resistance, execute the next play and drive into the end zone and score the touchdown, which in this case is equal pay. Unfortunately, the team did not execute the part of the plan that requires being *fully 100 percent committed* to the objective of equal pay.

Does Not Executing Equate to "Failure"?

So, was the team's effort a failure?

Absolutely not.

Unfortunately, the players' efforts to fully execute for equal pay were stymied by the human condition, a fact of life to which we are all subject. Before being faced with an existential challenge, none of us can predict what we're going to do when your very existence and ability to survive is challenged by a powerful institution.

No matter how vociferously we proclaim to possess the strength and toughness, none of us know what we're going to do when faced with extinction—especially if you have a choice over whether or not you will be extinguished.

In this instance, when staring their own career mortality in the face, these women made the decision to *exist* and keep their jobs and hard-earned spots on the US team—to be a living example for the young women who are coming after them, encouraging their successors to not be afraid to push forward to challenge the institution denying them the opportunity to be treated as equals.

When the USWNT's efforts are evaluated based upon their ability to handle and manage the human condition, these women should be applauded for the courageous efforts exerted to, with very limited resources, fight to the death, a huge and all-powerful institution.

That, in anyone's book, is execution.

Essentially, US Soccer challenged the USWNT's commitment to equal pay. Succinctly stated, the federation told the team that if the USWNT did not change the tone of the CBA negotiations and dilute their demand from "equal pay" to "fair and equitable pay," then on December 31, 2016, when the current MOU/CBA expired, US Soccer would seriously consider not extending operation of the MOU past its expiration, terminating their player contracts, eliminate their individual spots on the US team, take away their primary source of income, and effectively end their respective careers.

Essentially, US Soccer was daring the players to commit career suicide.

And the team blinked.

As a result, US Soccer penetrated the team's defensive line—the foundation of team unity, resolve, and commitment upon which the whole equal pay journey was predicated—and sacked the quarterback. The USWNT did not push back on US Soccer's ultimatums. On December 31, 2016, as time ran out on the clock, when the clock struck midnight, the team had abandoned their commitment.

In short, the team failed to *fully execute* on their 100 percent—do whatever it takes—commitment to secure equal pay. The USWNT did not reject USSF's threats of financial and career demise.

Instead, the team succumbed. The team changed the goal posts of their negotiations with the USSF. Keeping their jobs and only source of income ... in other words, financial survival suddenly became the immediate, existential goal. Acquiring "fair and equitable pay" instead of equal pay was now their objective.

In the red zone, faced with the choice of executing on their 100 percent commitment to equal pay or economic extinction, the USWNT succumbed to a very understandable human condition.

Survival.

As a result, no equal pay.

It is important to note that when faced with the existential threat of financial extinction—no income—these brave, strong, world champion women could only be stopped by the innate human need to survive.

Remember, US Soccer chose to threaten to rip away USWNT players' careers, jobs, incomes, and futures in the sport the women loved in order to force them to change the tone of the CBA negotiations and dismount from their relentless ride and quest for equal pay. All of this to drive the USWNT to instead settle for US Soccer's codified commitment to provide fair and equitable pay. The fact that US Soccer had to pull out all these stops should still be considered a monumental achievement for the women.

Importantly, *execution* is also doctrinally defined as the ability to have *accomplished*.

Arguably, the team did *accomplish* something novel and significant.

Specifically, the USWNT blazed a trail—a Lewis and Clark—type of path—to equality and equal pay that at no time in history had any woman or group of women in the active workforce ever attempted. Never had any group of women presented a legal challenge in which formal complaints were filed against their current employers—employers from whom the women received, and expected to continue to receive income albeit deficient, after suing the boss alleging wage discrimination in violation of Title VII and the 1963 Equal Pay Act.

At no time in history had any group of women in any industry had the temerity and guts to throw down the gauntlet and officially, legally, and very publicly accuse their employers of such egregious violations of the law in such a public fashion. Accordingly, with regard to the "accomplished" definition of execution, the US Women's National Soccer Team executed in spades.

Importantly, an opportunity did arise five months into the USWNT's equal pay CBA negotiations with US Soccer. As both sides awaited the federal court's decision as to whether or not the team could strike or boycott the 2016 Olympic Games, US Soccer presented the USWNT with its first and only economic counteroffer to the team's CBA equal pay proposal.

In mid-May 2016, two weeks prior to the federal court's ruling, the federation had finally provided us their first economic counteroffer to the initial CBA proposal for equal pay that we delivered to them in January 2016. Incredibly, after at least five in-person, New York City negotiation sessions that commenced in February 2016, US Soccer had failed to provide us a counteroffer.

But, the USSF did field a formidable negotiating team.

Unfortunately, but true to his reputation, US Soccer President Sunil Gulati was not among the USSF negotiators. We figured that he'd stick to his age-old, but tired tactic of letting his disciples do the initial dirty work, then much later in the negotiations when the USSF's stonewalling tactics elicited vitriol or just plain-old abject frustration and agitation from the players or their negotiators, Gulati would ride in, issue a proclamation or job-threatening false "choice" to the players, and exit stage left.

What he didn't know is that this time, I had a different ending in mind.

The federation's "no equal pay for the USWNT" top negotiators included President Bill Clinton's former secretary of health and human services, former president of the University of Miami, and president of the Clinton Foundation—USSF board member Donna Shalala; President Obama's former Chief White House Counsel Kathryn Ruemmler; Lisa Levine; USSF Chief Financial Officer Eric Gleason; USSF Chief General Manager Tom King, and USSF's long-time, outside counsel Russ Sauer from the Big Law firm Latham & Watkins. Surprisingly, the numbers they offered were pretty good. In fact, when it was all said and done with the calculations finalized, they were 80 percent of the way to equal pay—or about $2.4 million away. In essence, US Soccer had offered us the same pay-to-play system that the men enjoyed. At that time, in this pay-to-play system, the men were paid $17,625 if they won a game, $8,125 if they played to a draw, and $5,000 if they just showed up. So when the US Soccer Federation provided us a counteroffer that essentially offered the women $14,000 if they won a game, $7,000 if they played to a tie, and $5,000 if they showed up and lost the game, the federation was about 80 percent of the way to equal pay. All in all, this was a bona fide very good offer. But, it was not equal pay. The federation was asking these women to take a risk. You might ask what risk would they be taking? Well, at least three risks.

First, since US Soccer would not guarantee that they would continue to finance the fledgling NWSL and or pay the national team players to play in the NWSL, essentially the women on the national team had *one* job – playing for the US Women's National Soccer Team. Thus, this job was their only secure source of income. On the other hand the men had a primary source of income playing in the MLS or on an international club team that provided them the opportunity to earn substantial income every year.

On the other hand, if the USWNT adopted the pay-to-play system and the USSF decided to not schedule any games, the USWNT players would not make any money. The first risk for the women was that the Federation was in charge of scheduling games. Accordingly, there was no guarantee how many games the Federation would schedule for the women if we accepted this pay-to-play compensation system.

Historically in order to tamp down the popularity of the women's national team, after each Olympic or World Cup victory, the federation scheduled *less* than twenty games per year for the women's team in the years after Olympic and World Cup victories. In fact, in a couple of the CBA negotiation sessions in 2016, the federation referred to the years after Olympic and World Cup victories for the women as the period in which the USSF would plan to spend little to no money promoting the USWNT team. That strategy made no sense.

But what was clear was that the if federation decided it was not going to schedule any games for the women, they wouldn't. So, if we were to accept this pay-to-play $14,000 for a win system, if the USSF decided to not schedule games in the "dark years" (the USSF's description) in which the USSF planned to spend a little of no money promoting the team, the players on the USWNT *would have no income*. So we needed a guarantee that the federation would schedule at least twenty games per year for the women—which, given their penchant for winning, would certainly afford them the opportunity to earn well over $300,000 a year, or at a minimum $100,000 each year if they lost each of the twenty games they played.

This amount was the same amount of money, the equal amount of money, that a man would earn if they lost twenty games per year.

So I suggested in a counteroffer that the federation do one of two things to mitigate the risk of the Federation scheduling less than twenty games a year and the women earning no money as a result.

Our counteroffer: the federation could either guarantee that it would schedule a minimum of twenty games per year for the US Women's National Soccer Team, or guarantee that each of the twenty-four women on contract with the national team would earn a minimum of $100,000 a year.

Since the minimum amount of money the men could make per year was $100,000, to have an opportunity to earn equal minimum pay, the women needed a guarantee of at least twenty games per year, so they would pocket $100,000 annually if they lost all twenty scheduled games, which would be the same amount of money and equal amount of money at the men were and if they lost twenty games each year, or the federation could just merely guarantee to pay each player on the women's national team $100,000 a year.

I told the federation if they could agree to one of those guarantees, we would have a deal.

So in essence, twenty-four players guaranteed to be paid $100,000 a year—a total amount of $2.4 million a year guaranteed by US Soccer—and we would have a deal for equal pay.

On May 16 the federation indicated that they would consider this proposal. In fact, it was Kathryn Ruemmler, President Obama's former chief white house counsel, sitting across from me pondering our counteroffer, and after much thought, she finally said "We will consider your proposal." However, she said, since we were asking the federation to guarantee the payment of $100,000 per player per year, it's only fair that we present to the federation a plan of action that will take into account the financials involved in payments involved if a player was injured, got sick, on the injured reserve, got pregnant, or wasn't playing for whatever reason.

They asked us to come back by May 31 and present them with a plan of execution so they could do the financial calculations required to determine whether or not they could guarantee the $100,000 per year per player. We agreed to do that and with that I suggested that the meeting should be adjourned. We'd only been there for three hours that day and Kathryn asked why should we adjourn.

My response: I said, "Kathryn, this is the first time in six months that the federation has said that they would consider anything that we proposed. So for me that is huge progress and I did not want to push our luck today." So, McAfee, Rapinoe, Feher and I left Latham & Watkins's office in Midtown Manhattan feeling pretty good that day. In fact, we thought that we were two weeks away from a deal on equal pay.

Truth be told, much to our surprise, their substantive counteroffer was compelling. If we accepted it, it would provide the team pay equal to 80 percent of what the USMNT were being paid. That would be 80 percent more money than the USWNT had ever earned.

So, the team had to make a decision, do we stick to and continue to execute our plan and push for equal and not 80 percent of equal compensation, or do we accept their counter as a "victory"?

Essentially, both sides were rolling the dice. If the judge declared that indeed, the no strike/no boycott provision in the expired 2012 CBA was *not* incorporated into the existing MOU/CBA, the team could strike or boycott the upcoming 2016 Olympics. Accordingly, a favorable ruling would give the USWNT tremendous leverage, and would probably lead to an equal pay deal prior to the mid-June selection of the Olympic team. Conversely, if the judge ruled that the team could not boycott or strike, our leverage would be diminished. Predictably, the team quickly decided to stick with and continue to execute its equal pay plan.

Simply stated, the perennial World Cup and Olympic champion USWNT merely wanted the same compensation provided to the uncelebrated USMNT. That's all. A simple request ... demand ... and now, legal challenge.

"Execution" in Sports

Likewise, when one examines the definition of *execution* as it relates to performance in sports, it reads as follows:

To properly perform the fundamental moves or mechanics required for success.

This is an interesting definition for execution.

Arguably, when the unprecedented efforts of the US Women's National Soccer Team in the pursuit of equal pay are examined within the confines of the sports performance definition of execution, it could be said that the team did in fact properly perform the fundamental moves in the *mechanics, tactics, and strategies* required for success.

They did execute!

The team properly executed the leverage requirement.

The team properly executed and exhibited a tremendous display of guts in the quest for equal pay.

The team properly executed and performed the fundamentals required to develop and drop nuclear bombs during the CBA negotiations for equal pay.

But unfortunately, they fell short on execution with regards to *commitment* and succumbed to the final and potentially fatal *nuclear bomb* dropped by US Soccer that instinctively triggered the players' basic instincts and the facets of the human condition that compels us all to do whatever we must do to survive.

So as a result, when examining and determining whether or not the team satisfied the execution tactic, it must be said that the team did not fully satisfy that which was tactically required to completely carry out and accomplish equal pay.

But the team did fully execute with regard to *accomplishment.*

As noted above, the team's legacy accomplishment is imbedded in the blazed trails that women following in their footsteps can pursue, unimpeded, on their respective journeys to equal pay.

10

The Genesis of the RICO Case

Red Card

One player whose commitment to equal pay was undeniable and unshaken despite US Soccer's misappropriation of her job and career was Hope Solo. For Solo, despite her history of unexpected personal pain, getting fired by US Soccer was devastating. Mind-blowing. Surreal. Totally unexpected.

It was like being kicked out of the family. Many of the players did not support the players association acceding to Hope's request of them to file a grievance challenging her termination. Hope was essentially shunned by her former teammates.

Rich, they are going to fire me.

These are the words I heard Hope Solo scream to me on the phone about one week before US Soccer did in fact fire her.

Hope's premonition was foreign to me. For whatever reason, I didn't believe that US Soccer would fire the greatest goalkeeper of all time. Would they really cut off their nose to spite their face? Would they really terminate Hope Solo, the goalkeeper who had amassed 102 shutout performances?

I told Hope, *No way they fire you.*

It was about two weeks after Hope's comments about what she considered to be a coward's performance by the Swedish Olympic women's soccer team in its thrashing of the USWNT in the 2016 Olympic Games quarterfinals.

Knowing that the "coward" comments were not being well received here in the United States, on August 12 after the Swedish team defeated the women's team in the Olympic Games, Hope's manger, Melinda Travis and I virulently tried to convince her to either apologize for calling the Swedes cowards or indicate that her words were taken out of context.

True to the person that is Hope Solo, she refused to apologize because she meant what she said. She did say that her comments were probably taken out of context, that she didn't literally consider each player on the Swedish team to be a coward, but instead she thought their game strategy was cowardly. In essence, the Swedes did not bring the game to the United States, and Hope thinks that nonaggressive play is a coward strategy—which was the typical strategy deployed by Pia Sundhage, who was the Swedes' coach. In years past, Pia was head coach of the US Women's National Team and attempted to deploy the same kind of nonaggressivestyle of play—which was always rejected by the US Women's National Team.

Interestingly, what Melinda Travis and I did not know at the time was that Hope had had individual discussions with Sunil Gulati, and coach Jill Ellis on their flight home about her coward statements. Gulati and Ellis both told her not to worry about it, and that it wasn't a big deal. So, Hope didn't worry about it.

About ten days later, Hope unexpectedly got a call from Ellis telling her that they needed to meet with her as soon as possible. Having a great intuition with regard to the machinations of US Soccer, Hope knew that this was a strange kind of a meeting, and she just had the feeling that they were going to fire her. Thus, the call to me.

Hope wanted me to be at the meeting either in person or via telephone. Naïvely on my part, I told her I didn't think they were going to fire her and that if I showed up at the meeting it might antagonize them and cause negative stuff to transpire in the meeting so I suggested that Melinda attend with her, and I would participate via telephone. Hope agreed.

The meeting was relatively short. Dan Flynn, CEO of US Soccer, got right to the point. He basically said, "Hope, your contract has been terminated effective immediately for conduct unbecoming US Soccer, and you also will be suspended for six months effective immediately."

That was it! It lasted all of two minutes. I was kind of surprised. I asked whether or not the media had been alerted yet about this action, and they told me that they had not alerted the media. I also asked why the suspension was added to the termination, it didn't make any sense. I really never got an answer. But Lisa Levine did try to explain by saying, "Well, we needed the suspension just in case a new coach took over and wanted to call Hope in for tryouts—so if she's in suspended category for six months, Hope would not be able to even try out for the team, until February 2017 after serving the six-month suspension." Well, I thought, it makes a little sense but not much.

Hope was shocked. Needless to say, we were all very emotive. I received a call almost immediately from the *New York Times* asking for my comment about her suspension. I corrected the reporter and told him that Hope had been terminated from the US Women's National Soccer Team—she had been fired! Within minutes of my talking to the reporter, the *New York Times's* first iteration of an article appeared online. The headline indicated that Hope Solo had been suspended by US Soccer.

But what it really seemed like is that Hope Solo was fired in order to silence her and her demands and leadership on the team for equal pay. The USSF appeared to be sending a distinct message to the rest of the USWNT ... if we can fire the GOAT Hope Solo for persisting to want equal pay ... we can fire you too!!

True to her essence, Hope was going to fight what she considered to be an illegal retaliatory termination of her USWNT employment because of her relentless pursuit of equal pay. She filed her grievance against US Soccer and ultimately as USWNTPA counsel, Jeff Kessler represented her.

Likewise, if she was prohibited from pursuing equal pay as an insider on the USWNT, Hope would seek and pursue alternative vehicles through which she could pursue equal pay claims individually and on behalf of the team against US Soccer. Notably, despite being fired from the USWNT, Hope's EEOC complaint remained alive and well at the agency.

Unexpected Equal Pay Nuclear Weapon—RICO

In early 2017, Hope Solo and I began to receive random emails from Ken Bensinger, a journalist who claimed to be writing a book about soccer and wanted to interview us. At that time, Hope and I were still stinging from our startling and painful dismissals from the fight for equal pay that we orchestrated and then watched helplessly as the federation dropped its final and fatal nuclear bomb on the team and snuffed out any chance of getting equal pay in December 2016.

As we licked our wounds for several months, I didn't talk to Hope because I felt responsible for her ouster and pain, and she didn't talk with me because she felt responsible for mine. The last thing we wanted to do was to talk to a writer about soccer.

But, despite our snubs, as any good reporter would do, Bensinger persisted. Finally, in early 2018, shortly before his book *Red Card* was published, Bensinger called me. He was very polite. He explained that he had been calling me and Hope in hopes of being able to get us to endorse his book via a call-out on the cover. However, since the book was about to be released, it was too late for that opportunity.

But Bensinger did explain the premise of his work. Essentially, his book was a comprehensive soup to nuts review of the Department of Justice's RICO case and unprecedented prosecution of FIFA executives. Without revealing too much of the content, Bensinger offered to overnight me an advance copy of the tome to read and review. I accepted.

Now, the term *RICO* may sound familiar, and that probably has to do with the public's great amount of interest in the lives of mafia bosses, and now, the State of Georgia's indictment of former President Donald Trump on criminal RICO charges.

The Racketeer Influenced and Corrupt Organizations Act (RICO) is a complicated law that basically allows the government to file civil (for economic damages) and/or criminal cases to civilly pursue and/or criminally prosecute individuals who conspire to create rackerteering enterprise(s) designed to commit a predicate act or crime to pursue some economic benefit, or in furtherance of a criminal scheme(s). Crime bosses for a long time would have their subordinates carry out murders and other misdeeds on behalf of the criminal enterprise (the Mafia family), and in the end claim innocence as the bosses were not the ones to have committed the crimes. The RICO Law made it possible for authorities to go after bosses.

As promised, *Red Card* arrived on my Northern California doorstep very early the next morning. I opened the package immediately. With my morning cup of coffee in hand, I sat down and began to read.

In a word, the book was fascinating.

It's content just grabbed me. It was a page turner and absolutely riveting. Maybe not because it was that gripping of a story, but because Bensinger's description of FIFA, its executives, the way in which it operated and regarded its soccer (football) players and the business of the sport of soccer, was the mirror image of the United States Soccer Federation.

About two chapters in, Bensinger revealed that the DOJ's primary FIFA expert, target and ultimately its primary, most significant cooperator in the RICO probe was American soccer aficionado and FIFA executive committee and US Soccer board member Chuck Blazer. Interestingly, Blazer's protégé was Sunil Gulati, the president of the United States Soccer Federation.

Quite literally, the hair stood up on my neck.

Eureka!

As admitted by Blazer, FIFA was a racketeering criminal enterprise, a quintessential RICO organization. As Bensinger (via information provided to the DOJ by Blazer) described the inner workings of FIFA, the dictatorial reign of FIFA Chairman Sepp Blatter, the control Blatter exerted over FIFA's 160-plus country membership, and most importantly for my purposes, the way in which Blatter leveraged intimidation to control FIFA, was stunningly familiar.

Everybody kissed Blatter's ring!

As I continued to read Bensinger's work, I was struck by his thoroughness and attention to detail. More importantly, I was totally awed with Blazer's descriptions of how FIFA operated internally and externally. FIFA and the US Soccer Federation seemed to be mirror images of each other, in almost every way. When Bensinger described a FIFA operational function or activity, you could substitute US Soccer. When Bensinger described FIFA President Sepp Blatter's activities and dictatorial autocratic management style, I saw US Soccer's President Sunil Gulati. When Bensinger described the activities of FIFA's marketing agent "Traffic," I saw US Soccer's marketing agent Soccer United Marketing (SUM).

In sum, US Soccer was FIFA. FIFA was US Soccer. And they both appeared to operate on parallel paths. For a while, Blazer was the mastermind and driver of both entities. The similarities immediately triggered the notion that maybe, just maybe, US Soccer like FIFA was a RICO-like enterprise. The light bulbs went off in my head. In a civil-law context, if we could show that US Soccer was a racketeering enterprise which, in pursuit of enterprise economic benefits, it systematically invoked intimidation and loss of a job and spot on the USWNT to influence their individual and collective behavoir and elevate that behavior to a requisite RICO predicate act—to thwart the USWNT's efforts to achieve equal pay, we might have a mind-blowing, unprecedented RICO civil claim.

I was excited!

Accordingly, Solo's equal pay quest was not over. A civil RICO allegation would jolt the federation—hard. Just the prospect of a RICO claim would provide Solo leverage to settle her individual and the team's equal pay claims. I called Bensinger. I praised his work and promised to buy copies of his book for my friends and colleagues.

I also asked him if he could refer me to his RICO expert. He told me to call former United States Deputy Attorney General Jim Trusty.

I called Trusty immediately. Trusty (who at the time of this writing had just recently resigned from his representation of Former President Donald J. Trump in the classified documents case) had recently left the DOJ after more than twenty-five years of service—thirteen of which heading up the DOJ Division of Organized Crime & Gang Section and importantly, approving all DOJ civil and criminal RICO cases, including the DOJ's 2016 RICO case and successful prosecution of

FIFA executives—and was in private practice at a Washington, DC–based boutique white collar criminal defense law firm. To my surprise, Trusty answered his own phone.

That immediately scored points with me. A big-time lawyer answering his own phone. My immediate thought was he must be a good guy. And my initial impression was correct. I told Trusty who I was, who referred me to him, and why I was calling.

With great humility, Trusty very matter of factly told me his background. He also told me that his daughters were both huge fans of Hope Solo, and jokingly noted that being able to tell them that he talked to Hope Solo's lawyer today would score him huge points at home. Trusty invited me to come to DC to meet and talk about the equal pay case.

When I arrived at his office which is a stone's throw from the White House, I expected to be greeted by a pinstriped suit-wearing former deputy attorney general. Instead, I encountered a tall guy wearing an open collar white shirt, and loosened tie carrying an open can of Coke who welcomed me and motioned me to have a seat at the conference table in the firm's centrally located, three walls of glass conference room.

Trusty graciously gave me two hours of his time. I took him through the entire 2012 to 2016 equal pay journey. I explained how my thoughts of a prospective civil RICO claim against US Soccer were triggered by Bensinger's book and the remarkable similarities between the ways in which FIFA and the US Soccer Federation operate. FIFA was an alleged criminal RICO enterprise. Given the gross operational and leadership similarities, I proffered that the US Soccer Federation also operated like a RICO enterprise leveraging intimidation and fear of job loss against the players in order to "encourage" them to drop their pursuit of equal pay.

Absent the equal pay obligation, the federation would minimize the expense of "producing" its most valuable asset—the USWNT. The economic benefit derived from US Soccer's leveraging "intimidation" to cause the players to abandon their push for equal pay, while simultaneously selling that inexpensive asset (USWNT) into the television and corporate sponsorship marketplace at premium value and utilizing the financial proceeds to maximally fund the USMNT and Major League Soccer (MLS) was an intriguing value proposition.

If the federation's use of intimidation and threats of USWNT players' job loss qualified as a "predicate act" that activity would satisfy two objectives of a civil RICO enterprise. First, if intimidation caused the players to drop their economic equal pay demand, Players would remain on the team and thereby (a) preserve the teams' market value and cache, and (b) guarantee the longevity of the top quality, inexpensive, drastically underpaid USWNT "product" being sold by SUM into the marketplace at premium value.

Second, if intimidation and the fear of loss of their spot on the team if demands for equal pay persist "encourages" the players to abandon their quadrennial demands for equal pay, the costs of operating the USWNT would be kept at a minimum.

Thus, in theory, US Soccer is a civil RICO enterprise, and intimidation is elevated to the level of the predicate act, and the "scheme" is designed to guarantee the longevity, maintenance and low cost of producing and operating the federation's most valuable asset—the USWNT—while simultaneously leveraging the sale of the federation's World Cup and Olympic champion USWNT— its most successful, least expensive "asset," at a premium price via SUM to corporate sponsors and to multitudes of international and domestic television and digital broadcast entities.

Trusty was fascinated with my theory, but not convinced. He explained that alleging and then proving civil RICO was a complicated and tricky endeavor. Confidently, I told him that I had researched RICO and was almost certain we had a viable civil RICO claim. With that he instructed me to send him a draft RICO complaint.

In October 2019, I sent Trusty a ten-page skeleton draft of a RICO complaint against US Soccer. Much to my dismay, days and weeks went by before I received a response from Trusty. In the interim period, Trusty told me he was in trial and had not had a chance to critically review the draft complaint.

Finally, in late December 2019, Trusty called me to politely tell me—without laughing—that my draft complaint was woefully lacking in substance and needed a complete overhaul. I could tell that he really thought the draft was terrible, but his goodness as a human being and his perception of Hope and my commitment to equal pay and the seriousness of our pursuit of any available mechanism to extract equal pay from US Soccer caused him to offer to provide me a comprehensive thirty-five-page sample successful civil RICO complaint that he had drafted and utilized in successful pursuit of a civil RICO action, to utilize as a guide to draft a real RICO plaintiff's lawsuit. I accepted the offer and the challenge.

And what a challenge drafting a RICO complaint turned out to be. Over the next eight weeks, I dedicated four hours each morning to the painstaking construction of a RICO complaint. Utilizing Trusty's sample complaint as the roadmap and blueprint, paragraph by paragraph, page by page, line by line, word by word, I constructed the draft complaint.

Not once during this drafting period did I call Trusty. I was determined to demonstrate to him that I understood the facts of our case, and understood the complicated nuances of RICO well enough to weave together the pertinent elements of the RICO statute with the relevant facts to create a complaint that could survive a Rule 11 motion from US Soccer (the immediate dismissal of a complaint adjudged by the federal judge to be frivolous and without merit) and or a 12b(6) motion to dismiss.

Historically, civil litigants and plaintiffs' lawyers had abused the RICO statute and its prospects of treble damage awards by asserting frivolous RICO claims in a plethora of federal lawsuits. Additionally, RICO cases were complicated and took loads of court time to try. Federal judges were especially sensitive to any and all RICO filings. As a result, federal judges implored their extremely able and competent law clerks to closely peruse RICO complaints to make a quick determination of the seriousness and viability of the complaint. If the RICO allegations were weak, sloppy, and in the least bit stretched the notions of credulity and credibility, the judge would throw the case out and issue a Rule 11 order to sanction the lawyers that filed the frivolous RICO complaint.

Importantly, the defendant in a RICO case can also file Rule 11 motions to encourage the judge to dismiss the filing. Being hit with a Rule 11 sanction is the equivalent of being sent to the principal's office in full, professionally humiliating public view with a heavier cost to be paid by the offending lawyers than a school principal meted out to an offending student. Severe fines, public professional humiliation and if the infraction was doubly egregious, jail time was not out of the question. Accordingly, no lawyer wants to be "Rule 11'd" ever.

Once I was confident that I had a draft RICO complaint that I believed could survive a Rule 11 challenge, I sent it to Trusty. It was what I considered to be a comprehensive thirty-five-page, heavy-hitting indictment of US Soccer that quite succinctly illuminated the decades of psychological pain the federation inflicted on young women leveraging their hard work and dreams of ascending in their sport to a coveted spot on the United States Women's National Soccer Team. By invoking intimidation, coupled with constant covert and overt threats of losing that prized spot on the team if they refused to "toe the line" and submit to any and all demands and commands elicited by the United States Soccer Federation, including but not limited to dropping their quadrennial demands for equal pay, the federation maintained absolute dominion and control of the players on the USWNT. Additionally, as officially reported by Trusty's former DOJ colleague Sally Gates's investigation of allegations of sexual improprieties in 2021, that power and control was leveraged by executives and coaches in the form of sexual harassment and abuse of players in the US Soccer—created, financed, and controlled NWSL.

I believed the civil RICO complaint would represent a powerful indictment of the federation's unfettered use of the powerful workings of intimidation and fear of job and income loss and relinquishment of a spot on the USWNT—that final and dispositive nuclear bomb US Soccer dropped on the team in December 2016—to dislodge and defeat the team's commitment and quest for equal pay.

In the draft complaint, US Soccer's alleged use of intimidation, threats of being kicked off the team and loss of income, was the alleged all-important "predicate act" required—in a civil RICO claim—to sustain a civil RICO cause of action.

Several weeks passed before I heard back from Trusty. When he did call, he simply said that he'd like to work with me to dig deeper in an attempt to uncover enough facts to substantiate a pursuit of a civil RICO case.

Trusty noted that the draft complaint was strong, but we had two significant challenges. First, being able to succinctly describe the inner workings and the money flow of the alleged "racketeering enterprise" that the draft complaint alleged to be US Soccer, Soccer United Marketing, and MLS and compiling enough hard factual evidence of the federation's alleged use of intimidation and threats to players of loss of their jobs and spots on the USWNT to rise to the level of the requisite predicate act was going to be tough to do. But Trusty believed the facts to be strong enough for us to engage in a deep dive of fact-finding in an attempt to substantiate the claim.

With that, the race to RICO was on. For me and Hope, simply being able to leverage the inclusion of Trusty on our legal team and to at some point be able to communicate the prospect of Hope's filing of a RICO claim to US Soccer and then to the world would provide us and the team tremendous leverage to force the federation to settle our respective equal pay cases.

For decades, intimidation, threat of loss of your spot on the team, and loss of your only source of income—these were the emotional and psychological silent weapons US Soccer deployed to control the demands and very existence of players on the USWNT. In short, do what you're told, don't make waves, and definitely do not ask for equal pay and your spot on the team, and your paltry income will be safe. Acquiesce and you'll keep your job on the USWNT.

In the context of a potential RICO claim, was the Federation's intimidation prolific enough to constitute a defined RICO predicate act?

At the commencement of CBA negotiations in each of 2004, 2012, and 2016, the USWNT always issued demands to the defendant, USSF for equal pay. Indeed, historically, whether the USWNT elicited its equal pay demand before, during, or after collective bargaining negotiations, USSF rejected the USWNT players' demands for equal pay through the presence of Sunil Gulati. Our RICO theory of the case alleged that in order to carry out its civil RICO scheme, the US Soccer Federation continually engaged in a protracted, most times covert and unspoken pattern of intimidation, and threats to players that they may lose their jobs and roster spots on the World Cup or Olympic teams, or for those so-called "floater" players on the "bubble," the possibility of being denied opportunities to become members of the USWNT if they did not act per the directives and/or desires of the federation.

In order to maintain and perpetuate dominion, influence, and control of the psyche of USWNT players, according to several players, Gulati would often place random telephone calls to various players invoking conversations the innuendo and content of which made it clear to the player(s) that their jobs and or prospective roster spots on the World Cup and or Olympic teams could be in jeopardy. That is, if the players' individual and collective positions on various issues impacting the USWNT (e.g. compensation, venue and practice facility playing surfaces, etc.) did not ultimately comport with the federation's position on those matters, your spot on the team could be in jeopardy.

Gulati's telephone calls to individual players always elicited uneasiness, apprehension, intimidation and the feeling that their respective jobs and roster spots were at stake if they provided the wrong response to any of Sunil's questions, or if they expressed opinions different than that desired by the Gulati or the federation. After a matter-of-fact admonition from me, and a reminder that his calls to players constituted individual unfair labor practices, Gulati temporarily stopped making the calls in December 2015.

Several players recounted their personal experiences when placed in the unenviable position of being on the receiving end of a Gulati call.

Player 1

Around 2013, despite a stellar collegiate career and attendance at multiple USWNT top-level training camps, Player 1 was not selected to be a member of the USWNT. Frustrated by her non-selection, she decided to go abroad to play for a foreign professional soccer team in order to get paid and to hone her skills by getting more top-level international competitive playing time. Within a few weeks of her joining the foreign team, US Soccer through President Gulati contacted Player 1 via telephone and with great, unmistakable determination, "encouraged" her to come back home to play for the USWNT. Reading between the lines, it was clear to the player that this was not an "ask," it was a *demand*.

Citing her recent, still raw wounds from being summarily rejected three times in her attempts to make the USWNT, her contractual professional commitment to play for the foreign team, and her ability to play more and earn about the same money playing overseas, Player 1 declined the offer to return to the USA to play for the USWNT. The call ended politely, but with a tinge of trepidation.

Less than twenty-four hours after Gulati's first call, he called again. This time, on behalf of US Soccer, Gulati was forceful, intimidating, and direct. Gulati told the Player that this would be her last chance to ever be on the USWNT.

Fearing that Gulati and the federation would make good on their threats of lifetime banishment from the USWNT, the player relinquished her lucrative job on the foreign team, and as a result of the intimidation and threats of never being able to realize her lifelong dream of playing for the USWNT, she quit the foreign team, abandoned the opportunity for extensive, skill-honing playing time, and returned to play for the low-paying USWNT.

The 2015 World Cup victory did operate to ameliorate some of the pain she experienced as a result of US Soccer's intimidation tactics, but Gulati lived on in full view. Having had success leveraging intimidation tactics with this player, in December 2016, shortly after the EEOC's "the federation may be culpable" call with the federation, reportedly, Gulati descended upon several USWNT players and strongly suggested that when all the existing CBA (an "MOU") and USWNT players' contracts expired on December 31, 2016, they'd all lose their jobs on that day, unless, they among other things, abandoned their current demands for equal pay, and instead just have conversations about equal pay, immediately change the tone of their CBA negotiations and adopt a more collaborative versus combative attitude, and ultimately agree to and accept "fair and equitable pay" instead of equal pay in the next CBA or risk losing their jobs and their spots on the USWNT.

Under extreme duress, the USWNT succumbed to US Soccer and, on or about December 31, 2016, in fear of losing their jobs and only secure source of income, USWNT players abandoned their quest for equal pay.

Player 2

Player 2 is a longtime member of the USWNT. Over many years, she participated in formal and informal discussions with Gulati and various US Soccer representatives about USWNT compensation and general playing conditions. She always told Gulati and the federation that the USWNT wants equal pay and equal treatment.

Player 2 describes the environment created and perpetuated by US Soccer as the "bully system," and she offers that to withstand Gulati's seemingly constant intimidation, the USWNT players needed to be strong women. With regard to Gulati's response to Player 2's informal and formal demands for equal pay, Gulati would always respond, "No. This is all you're getting."

Player 2 notes that notwithstanding the USWNT's success and her protests about the lack of equal pay, Gulati and US Soccer's position with regard to their compensation was, "It is what it is. Take it or quit and go get another job." According to Player 2, intimidation and the constant threat of job loss were the normal environment in which Player 2 and the USWNT players existed.

Player Trades

In the inaugural NWSL season, USWNT players had the right to select the NWSL city/team for which they would play. The players believed that per the March 2013 MOU, if after each season, an NWSL team wanted to execute a trade for a USWNT player with another NWSL team, the federation and the USWNT players agreed that the player would have the right to *consent* or *reject* a trade. Remember, the 2013 MOU codified and committed the USWNT players to provide their professional services to NWSL teams to which they were assigned by the federation.

In September 2014, after the second NWSL season, a few players were traded to other NWSL teams. The traded players informed US Soccer that they objected to and rejected the trade. The federation told them that they did not have the right to object to the trades. The USWNT teammates of the traded players and the USWNTPA supported the traded players' position.

In early 2015, a few months before the traded players had to report to their respective new NWSL team training camps, the traded players and the USWNTPA were contemplating filing an official grievance to challenge the efficacy of the trades.

To be clear, the trade language in the MOU was a bit ambiguous. Specifically, the Federation commits to coordinate with a USWNT Player(s) about their respective NWSL team situations and exert its best efforts to trade a Player if US Soccer and the Player agreed that a trade was in order. Given this language, all of the USWNT players believed they each had the right to "not agree" to a trade.

In or about February 2015, one month away from the players' obligations to report to NWSL team training camps, and a couple of months before the federation's selection of players for the 2015 World Cup team, one of the traded players received a telephone call from Gulati on behalf of US Soccer in which Gulati strongly insinuated that if the traded players continued to challenge their respective NWSL trades, these players may not be selected to the World Cup team. As noted above, at that time in February 2015, pursuant to USWNT players' rights promulgated in the MOU between the USSF and the USWNTPA, the players had the right to consent or reject a trade, and, on behalf of them, the USWNTPA was poised to file a formal grievance against the USSF to invoke that right.

After the frightful, intimidating and what the traded player perceived to be a warning-type telephone call from Gulati, the player immediately contacted the USWNTPA, relayed the content of the call, and instructed them to immediately (a) cease any and all communication with US Soccer or the NWSL about the NWSL player trades, and (b) abandon the pursuit of the grievance to challenge their trades to alternate NWSL teams.

Once again, in order to preserve their pending opportunity to be selected to the 2015 World Cup Team, the traded players abandoned a negotiated contractual right to determine upon which team they would be employed in the US Soccer's NWSL.

Equal Play, Equal Pay T-Shirts, and Facial Stickers

In July 2016, one month prior to the 2016 Rio Olympic Games, the team embarked upon a series of friendly (invitational matches against international soccer teams) competitions. The USWNT determined that it should leverage the media and public support for their quest for equal pay during the friendly matches prior to the Olympic Games.

Accordingly, the team created "equal pay" apparel (e.g. T-shirts and facial sticker tattoos emblazoned with "#Equal Play Equal Pay"). The plan was for the USWNT players to wear the T-shirts and face tattoo stickers emblazoned with EQUAL PLAY EQUAL PAY in the team's hotels prior to the friendly matches, and during the team friendly pre-game warm-ups. Unfortunately, US Soccer's game-time apparel rules prohibited wearing anything but official US Soccer uniform game-time wear before and during the games. Otherwise, the players would have affixed the stickers to their faces and worn the T-shirts during the televised pregame warm-ups and during the games.

On the day before the mid-July 2016 friendly match, the *New York Times* published an article on the team's equal pay battle with the USSF. The article was accompanied by a photograph of the top five players—Hope Solo, Alex Morgan, Megan Rapinoe, Carli Lloyd, and Becky Sauerbrunn—that had filed EEOC complaints against the USSF wearing the "Equal Play Equal Pay" T-shirts.

Accordingly, Solo and several members of the USWNT planned to wear those same T-shirts—in full public view—as they walked from the hotel lobby to board the bus to the game. Thus, players were wearing the T-shirts in the USWNT's specially designated hotel dining room in the hours prior to boarding the team bus for the ride to the stadium.

However, during the hour prior to the team's scheduled departure from the hotel to the stadium, Hope Solo called to tell me that Gulati appeared unexpectedly in the team dining room. Solo indicated that Gulati approached each and every player wearing the Equal Play Equal Pay T-shirt and allegedly communicated that unspecified disciplinary action would ensue if they wore the T-shirts or the facial tattoo stickers during the short walk from the hotel lobby to and/or on the team bus, or at or near the game.

Despite their pledge to promote their equal pay quest on the pitch in full view of the television cameras and audience, no USWNT player wore an equal pay T-shirt or facial tattoo sticker on the walk from the hotel lobby to the team bus, or for that matter, ever again.

Hope Solo Squeezed Too!

In 2014, Hope Solo had a highly publicized skirmish with her half-sister and nephew in Washington State. Subsequently, Solo was charged with two misdemeanor counts of assault, and pled not guilty to the charges. Solo's counsel filed several motions including a motion to dismiss which were granted in January 2015.

However, in a rare move, the prosecution appealed the dismissal of the charges. At the outset of the June 2015 World Cup, the appeal of the dismissal of the charges were pending in a Washington State Superior Court.

On a Sunday, two days before the USWNT's first 2015 World Cup tournament game, ESPN's *Outside the Lines* broadcast an over-the-top, salacious negative story about Solo's pending case. Two days later, despite ESPN's troubling broadcast, and a torrent of negative media, Solo and the USWNT won their first 2015 World Cup match.

Notwithstanding Solo's stellar performance in the first World Cup match, the ESPN broadcast caused the media and US Senator Richard Blumenthal to pressure US Soccer to kick Solo off the team. The senator's pressure on US Soccer to immediately jettison Solo from the team was so intense that I immediately assembled a legal team comprised of crack litigators that included Dallas-based attorney Paul Stafford and Art McAfee to be prepared to pursue an emergency arbitration the next day to thwart the termination if the federation caved and kicked Solo off the World Cup team. The USWNT's next match would be conducted five days later on the following Sunday. Mercifully, US Soccer ignored the senator and the media and did not terminate Solo.

However, on Saturday morning, one day before the USWNT's second game in the 2015 World Cup tournament, Solo was summoned to the hotel room of the USSF's CEO, Dan Flynn. When she arrived, Solo was met by Flynn and the USSF's top outside lawyer, Russ Sauer. They told Solo they wanted to question her about her pending domestic violence case in Washington State that had been the subject of the ESPN broadcast.

Solo told them that she had been advised by her lawyer that in order to preserve the attorney-client privilege, she should not disclose any information about her pending case to third parties.

Demonstrating the USSF's continued use of intimidation, and threat of job loss, prospective loss of Solo's primary source of income, and immediate loss of Solo's job and banishment from the World Cup competition, the federation's CEO and top lawyer told Solo that if she refused to cooperate and refused to divulge to them the confidential, attorney-client privileged protected information about her then pending domestic violence prosecution, she might be immediately terminated from then USWNT and the World Cup competition.

Fearing that, Solo succumbed to the threats and intimidation, relented and, contrary to the advice of her personal counsel, to keep her job and spot on the World Cup team, put herself in possible legal jeopardy in her criminal case, potentially waived the attorney-client privilege, and talked to the CEO and USSF lawyer about her pending case.

Clearly, even the decidedly strongest player on the team fell victim to the strong-arm tactics exerted by the federation. When faced with intimidation and prospective income and job loss—nine times out of ten, humans will choose survival.

PART III

11

The Aftermath and a Warning for the Future

SACKED IN THE red zone.

Super Bowl victory denied.

Despite a concentrated, pressure-packed, valiant, and historic run at achieving equal pay in 2016, US Soccer sacked the United States Women's National Team just short of the goal.

With the threat of the termination of their player contracts, loss of paltry slave wage-type income, and the expiration of their MOU/CBA on December 31, 2016, if they chose to push forward in the quest for absolute equal pay, the players opted for the safe option, to survive.

The US Soccer Federation and the extremely weakened USWNT entered into negotiations for a new CBA in January 2017. At this point, the USWNT was devoid of leverage and under extreme economic duress to get a new compensation deal done by the federation's April 1, 2017 deadline, and incredulously under the new players association leadership of Becca Roux, McKinsey's young analyst.

Remarkably, in the person of Roux, the federation had effectively installed McKinsey, its famed and powerful management consultant, to be in control of the players association. In order for the players to continue to get paid until a new CBA was secured, US Soccer gifted the players—per the federation's right when CBA's expire—by electing to continue the operation of the expired MOU and the issuance of paychecks to the players into 2017.

But, notwithstanding the concession, the federation reportedly informed the players that the extension of that MOU and their ability to get paid would last only up until April 1, 2017. If the players association and the federation didn't have a CBA deal for fair and equitable pay—not equal pay—by April 1, there would be no deal and all the players could be terminated.

Essentially, the USWNT were US Soccer's hostages until April 2017.

Technically, Roux was selected by the players to assume the leadership of the USWNT Players Association as its new executive director. At the behest of client US Soccer and under the guise of offering young, impressionable USWNT players professional guidance with regard to the development of the players association for free, Roux befriended a few USWNT players in late 2015 and began the slow but deliberate process of disengaging the players' trust in their players association leadership and diluting the push for and ultimately eroding the players' commitment to equal pay.

Roux first physically appeared on the scene at a players association meeting in Los Angeles in the first week of January 2016, a few days after the they submitted their equal pay CBA proposal to US Soccer. Apparently, probably as early as November 2015, McKinsey & Company in the person of Roux had been in contact with a few players who were on the proverbial bubble with regard to their projected longevity on the team.

US Soccer and McKinsey's objective was to infiltrate the players association and dismantle their unity around equal pay by planting seeds of distrust and painting USWNTPA leadership (Art McAfee and me) as weak and lacking the skills, knowledge, and ability to develop their players association into an effective organization. US Soccer via McKinsey was deploying classic union-busting tactics proscribed by one of the most powerful management consulting companies in the world to defeat the USWNT's quest for equal pay.

That's how important it was for US Soccer to deny equal pay to the team.

The comprehensive objective was to infiltrate the union with spies, co-opt weak players, discredit union leadership, and slowly but surely destroy the team's unity from within. Essentially, US Soccer knew that if they could disengage the teams' power base which was the players' unity, and successfully divide and conquer, the federation would eventually dismantle the players' commitment to equal pay.

I was not made aware of Roux's presence until a couple of days before the players association meeting in Los Angeles in early January 2016. One of the older players on the team decided to let me know that the team had invited Roux and a colleague to attend the meeting to make a presentation about marketing and group licensing—two subjects that McAfee and I would learn that Roux and her colleague knew nothing about.

I was a bit shaken and disappointed that the players would invite outsiders to our meeting without letting me know, but it's the players' organization and they can do whatever they want. It was also an indication that despite my engagement of famed sports lawyer Jeffrey Kessler, some of the players were still inclined to believe that McAfee and I did not have the chops to make it happen.

When the meeting convened, in order for us to have a confidential discussion about our CBA proposal, we invited Roux and her partner to present first. Roux thanked the players for inviting them and noted that they looked forward to partnering with the players association (PA)— pro bono—to help grow the players union. She noted that they would commence by helping them develop a marketing and group licensing plan (GLP).

Notably, Art McAfee and I had already alerted the players that we were developing a plan that mimicked the NFLPA program. In fact, we included some of the basic lucrative economic triggers of our contemplated GLP into the CBA proposal we had delivered to the federation a few days before Roux's presentation.

More interestingly, not long after Roux and her colleague attempted to explain the workings of a GLP, the untutored and clearly flustered Roux acknowledged that she was not equipped to explain the workings of a GLP and asked me and Art to assist her presentation.

In order to appear to be going along with the players' program of embracing outside expert McKinsey's assistance in proliferating marketing and group licensing capabilities of the players association, Art—who for seventeen years as senior counsel with the NFLPA oversaw the operations of its lucrative GLP program—and I graciously assisted and as the true experts, explained how to create, operate, leverage, and manage a group licensing plan that could generate millions of dollars for the USWNTPA.

When the marketing and GLP discussion concluded, Roux and her partner left the meeting so that we could conduct the confidential business of the PA.

Art and I did not learn that McKinsey was in fact the governance management consultant to the US Soccer Federation until early April 2016, in a *Wall Street Journal* article about corporate governance.

Since Roux was still seemingly ever-present with the players, upon being made aware that the federation was a McKinsey client, I immediately reached out to the McKinsey general counsel and pursued an official engagement letter between the PA and McKinsey. Knowing that McKinsey's conflicting client relationship with the federation would probably prohibit McKinsey from taking us on as an official client—absent the players association executing a conflict waiver or McKinsey's disengagement of their representation of the federation—the clear conflict of interest would render McKinsey unable to sign the engagement letter to represent us too.

For a variety of reasons, McKinsey silently declined the execution of an official engagement letter.

By late April, Roux seemed to have disappeared. The immediate threat of union busting dissipated.

At least for the time being.

I was certain that at the first sign of a crack in the armor of team unity, McKinsey in the person of Roux would reappear.

That time came on September 1, one week after US Soccer fired Hope Solo.

With a little more than three months to go before the December 31 expiration of the MOU and their player contracts, the federation had sent a silent but very clear warning to the players: If US Soccer could kill the job and career of Hope Solo, they too could be annihilated.

Roux's Reign

In January 2017, in a deceptive show of full strength, the entire team engaged in the new CBA negotiations with the federation. It was essentially an optics exercise to mask the internal chaos that reportedly engulfed the players and Roux.

By all accounts, it was a disaster. US Soccer assumed its pre-2016 strong-arm, dictatorship-like style of negotiation and dictated the take it or leave it CBA terms to which the federation was prepared to agree.

It was ugly, but the team put on a brave face. They did not have much of a choice.

The one-way negotiations ended around April 4, 2017, in the Chicago offices of US Soccer when Gulati reportedly presented what he characterized as his final CBA offer to the team, left the meeting, jumped into a car, called the players from the car and told them they had from that moment until he arrived at O'Hare to catch a flight to accept or reject the offer.

Under extreme pressure the team agreed to a terrible CBA. Not only did the new four-year CBA eliminate at least eight contracted jobs on the team (reduction from twenty-four contracted jobs to sixteen by the end of the CBA) but also it lowered guaranteed income for the non-star players, reduced bonus opportunities, and most importantly, the players lost power.

When the deal was announced, the team expressed satisfaction. But one has to believe that the veterans knew they got screwed. But, the team was hopeful that the federation would come to recognize their status as the USSF's most valuable asset and ultimately treat and compensate them accordingly. However, it did not take long to realize that a leopard (US Soccer Federation) does not change its spots.

Recognizing that they had squandered an opportunity to grab equal pay and had instead settled for a terrible compensation structure that was neither fair or equitable, the players quietly placed their hope for equal pay salvation in the still ongoing EEOC investigation.

At the end of their prioritized intense eight-month investigation of the Solo, Morgan, Sauerbrunn, Lloyd, and Rapinoe complaints, in early December 2016, in separate same-day calls to the players and USSF representatives, with one glaring caveat, the EEOC proclaimed that their preliminary conclusion was that US Soccer had violated the Equal Pay Act.

However, before cementing that conclusion into a formal charge against US Soccer for violating the Equal Pay Act and Title VII wage discrimination, the EEOC indicated to the players that the EEOC needed the players' help getting the EEOC's arms around US Soccer's defense that the USMNT accrued more revenue than the USWNT—an argument that provided US Soccer a legal defense to claims that they violated the Equal Pay Act and allowed them to legally not provide women equal pay.

Essentially, it is legal to pay women less than a man doing the same job if the reason for paying females less is something other than their sex. Accordingly, US Soccer falsely asserted that the USWNT earned less revenue for the federation than the USMNT. As a result, the federation claimed it was legal to pay the USWNT less.

Incredibly, the United States government was asking the players to help them get what we had already provided them—evidence that the USWNT accrued more revenue than the USMNT. In fact, the evidence we provided the EEOC was the same 2015 US Soccer financials that clearly showed that in fiscal year 2014-15, the USWNT produced $20 million in revenue with an operating profit of $17 million, and the USMNT accrued $5 million with an operating loss of $2 million. When we proudly produced these US Soccer financials and waved them in the faces of US Soccer's negotiators during a March 15, 2016 CBA negotiating session, Russ Sauer blurted out that those "financials" to describe the results which Sauer declared was an "aberration".

The problem with that characterization was that in its pro forma financial projections, US Soccer showed that the USWNT was, by US Soccer's own projections, slated to continue to annually accrue more revenue than the USMNT at least through fiscal year 2019. We had the federation dead to rights. We had dismantled their only legitimate reason for not agreeing to equal pay. We told them so in their faces during negotiations. Yet, they would not budge from their position. In fact, the negotiators wouldn't even talk about the verity of their own financials.

Totally frustrated after several hours of staring at the unresponsive faces of US Soccer's negotiators, without warning, I instinctively and abruptly turned my chair around and started talking to the wall behind me in the conference room. I indicated that it was much more productive and less disappointing to talk to the wall than to the USSF representatives because I didn't expect a response from the wall which tempered the disappointment I felt when talking to the USSF negotiators from whom I at least expected the courtesy of a response.

When I turned around, the USSF folks were pissed off. Art was desperately trying not to laugh, and Rapinoe and David Feher just stared straight ahead. Frankly, at that juncture, the level of abject disrespect we had endured during three CBA negotiation sessions that included several incidences of eye rolling from Russ Sauer almost every time I talked that became so pronounced and prolific that after one eye roll I leaned on the table and starred into Sauer's eyes and dared him to do it again. The venom was so pronounced from me that Sauer responded with a decidedly sharp remark that my seething somehow didn't allow me to hear. But Donna Shalala heard it and so did Art McAfee, who, without missing a beat, told Sauer that the there was no need to be disrespectful or something to that effect. Shalala, to her immense credit, was so incensed at Sauer's comment that she physically rushed to our side of the table to discern whether or not we were okay, Shortly thereafter, the meeting adjourned for the day.

KNOWING THAT WITH the election of Donald Trump, their tenure was about to end, the EEOC encouraged the players and US Soccer to engage in an EEOC-hosted mediation before the end of December to resolve the equal pay claims. Neither the players nor the federation responded to the EEOC's offer. At the end of December 2016, the historic Solo, Morgan, Rapinoe, Lloyd, and Sauerbrunn EEOC claims remained open and unresolved.

The EEOC went silent.

At the end of the Obama presidency, the Trump administration took control of the EEOC and certainly, equal pay for women in any workplace including the soccer pitch was not a priority. As a result, for the entire year of 2017, we did not hear a peep from the EEOC.

Finally, in March 2018, in response to several cordial "what is the status of the EEOC" investigation inquiries from the team's and Hope Solo's lawyers (me), the Trump EEOC reappeared.

Essentially, after one year of absolute silence, the EEOC told us that they had not reviewed their predecessor's investigation or its results, and they were not going to perform that exercise. In fact, they indicated that they were not going to do anything on the case.

Incredulously, short of rekindling the investigation, the Trump EEOC asked us what did we want them to do?

First, we decided to leverage the power of their agency and its optically available opportunity to continue the pursuit of our claims and rule that the federation violated the Equal Pay Act. We wanted to leverage the power of the federal government to compel the US Soccer Federation to come to the table and settle our equal pay and Title VII wage discrimination claims. Thankfully, the EEOC agreed to be that conduit.

Accordingly, per guidelines provided in Title VII and the Equal Pay Act, we calculated a back pay settlement demand that if accepted by the federation would provide upwards of $60 million to the players for US Soccer's 2013 to 2016 violations of the EPA and Title VII.

In mid-April 2018, the EEOC delivered our settlement demand to the federation.

Basically, "fuck you" was US Soccer's almost immediate and figuratively audible response.

Subsequently, in July 2018, the EEOC reiterated that short of reviewing and or continuing the investigative work and conclusions of their Obama equal pay proponent predecessors—which they indicated they were not going to do—they again noted that they were poised to do what we asked of them. Legally, the only options remaining were the EEOC's issuance of No Action and Right to Sue letters to each of the five players that filed EEOC complaints, or absent any edict or commentary, issuance of right to sue US Soccer letters to each of the five complainants.

What had been a historic, powerful, groundbreaking, potentially game-changing action that was poised to forever disrupt the stayed no equal pay for women in the workforce reality—specifically, the alleged US Soccer Federation violations of the Equal Pay Act and wage discrimination under Title VII that risked the five EEOC complaintants' jobs, income, reputations, and careers—had now, after a blistering battle in 2016, devolved into silence from the EEOC.

Not one to wait around to be led, on August 24, 2018, Hope Solo filed the first lawsuit against the US Soccer Federation alleging violations of the Equal Pay Act and wage discrimination under Title VII.

Solo asked the team to join her lawsuit. To this day, Solo awaits a response from them.

We could only surmise that they were banking beyond hope that the federation would come to its senses and realize that the terms of the terrible but active 2017 CBA were egregious and unfair.

However, in November 2018, I was made aware that the players were done with the unfair treatment by the federation and were preparing to file their own equal pay litigation against US Soccer. Accordingly, by March 8, 2019, the players realized they had been duped yet again by signing that abysmal 2017 CBA with the federation and filed a class action federal lawsuit in the Central District Court of California that mirrored Solo's equal pay litigation filed nine months earlier.

At this stage, the previously younger players were now older veterans in the cycle, had shed their "just happy to be here" mentality, and were suffering from the 2017 CBA's terrible compensation metrics.

Quite surprisingly, in May 2020 the trial court opined that over an aggregated five-year period, the USWNT had actually earned more money than the USMNT and abruptly dismissed the USWNT's class action lawsuit in which the team alleged that the US Soccer Federation had engaged in wage discrimination and violated the Equal Pay Act and Title VII.

Believing the court's ruling to be erroneous, the Team appealed the trial court's decision to the Ninth Circuit Court of Appeals. However, instead of litigating the appeal of the dismissal, or joining Solo's then, still active equal pay lawsuit in federal court in Northern California, in February 2022, the USWNT decided to take matters into their own hands and settle their litigation for $24 million—$5.5 million of which was dispersed to pay the team lawyers. The remainder of the litigation settlement proceeds were distributed via a formula created by the team finance expert.

It's very important to understand and accept that the team settled the litigation. The settlement did *not* provide them an award of equal pay.

In the settlement, US Soccer merely *pledged* to provide equal pay in the future, if and when the USWNT satisfies three conditions.

First, in order for US Soccer to provide the USWNT equal pay, the USWNT and the USMNT must enter into a joint collective bargaining agreement with US Soccer.

Second, FIFA must agree to provide the men's and women's teams that win the World Cup equal prize money.

Third, the USWNT and USMNT must agree on what comprises an equal rate of pay as that term is defined in the Equal Pay Act. For a variety of reasons, all three of these conditions will *never* be satisfied by the USWNT.

As a result, the closest thing the USWNT could get to equal pay was to agree to accept the men's pay-to-play compensation system in their new 2022 CBA and sell that as equal pay to the world.

It's not.

12

Women in Other Industries Talking of Their Battles for Equal Pay

IN APRIL 2016, Pam Greenwalt, SAG-AFTRA's director of communications and SAG-AFTRA executive director Duncan Crabtree-Ireland reached out to me and offered the USWNT whatever support and help the actors union could provide in our quest for equal pay. Certainly, it was no secret that equal pay for women in the business of acting was a long-sought-after objective. Ms. Greenwalt noted that SAG-AFTRA was closely monitoring our (USWNT) tactics and progress in our equal pay fight. The Hollywood inveterate conglomerate of movie and television studio juggernauts that hindered female actors' ability to receive equal pay was not unlike our Goliath—the US Soccer Federation.

In a show of solidarity with the USWNT, the actors in the famed television show *Grey's Anatomy* wore our "Equal Pay Equal Play" T-shirts on the set of the show. If we were successful, SAG-AFTRA wanted to mirror our equal pay blueprint.

Notably, the equal pay tactics we deployed (leverage, guts, nuclear options, commitment, and execution) were applicable in SAG-AFTRA's situation. However, the big challenge for SAG AFTRA in the year 2023 was their ability to establish leverage.

Typically, to establish leverage, workers can stop working, withhold professional services, and halt the generation of the "results" of the services they provide. Leverage meant no professional services, no product, and no revenues for management. It also resulted in no income for the professional service providers (e.g. employees, actors, soccer players).

SAG AFTRA workers (actors) and their affiliated professional service provider unions (e.g. stunt actors, editors, grippers, camera and sound providers, etc.) produce content (films, TV shows). If there's no "content" to deliver to the movie and television studios to sell to the movie and television content distributors (e.g. CBS, NBC, ABC and Streaming Services) and then to sell to the consuming public (viewers), that typically leads to leverage for SAG/AFTRA.

No actors, no content.

However, in this new, ever-evolving era of streaming intertwined with cross-ownership and/or license rights to distribute existing content over many broadcast mediums, most importantly, streaming platforms (e.g. Netflix, Amazon Prime, Hulu, etc.), the availability of pre-strike existing content to fill the air-time reserved for new content—dampened and diluted the actors' ability to gain leverage by withholding their professional services. Old existing content that was licensed to streaming services long before the actor strike, was used to fill the void that the lack of new content left behind. Even though the actors were not producing new content, the studios and broadcast platforms still had products to *sell* to consumers.

Unlike professional sports—for instance, soccer where *live* games are the *new* content, and in which the possibility of player strikes, boycotts, or the prospect of some other form of temporary work stoppage can create *leverage* for the performers (professional athletes)—in film and TV, new content is no longer required to keep the studios and broadcasters' money-making engines running. Instead, old existing content can sustain their broadcast content needs for the foreseeable future—a fact that severely undercut SAG/AFTRA's ability to create *leverage* via a strike.

Notwithstanding those realities, at some point re-watching episodes of their favorite shows on various streaming services got *old* and the demand for new content from striking actors reigned supreme. The question was, how long can actors, stunt professionals, and production workers afford to be without work?

It's the age-old question and challenge in labor/management disputes about compensation.

Would the various industry professionals' need for income slowly dissolve their commitment and resolve to fight for equal pay before the consuming public's demand for new content forces the film and television broadcast studios to cave and provide equal compensation?

Would the professionals have the guts required to continue to withhold content production services?

Does SAG/AFTRA have any nuclear bombs to drop on the studios?

Would the union members sustain their *commitment* to strike?

Finally, would SAG/AFTRA have total union membership commitment to fully *execute* their work-stoppage to get equal pay plan?

It all remained to be seen. The fact that all aspects of the television and film industry (content creation, distribution models, mechanisms and mediums, pricing of content development and costs of distribution, direct-to-consumer channels, independent content development, and distribution) literally changed overnight severely complicated the situation, and made it almost impossible for the three sides—content developers, actors, and studios—to predict costs and profitability. These factors are needed in order to negotiate an economically fair labor/management deal.

Ultimately, the existence of the television and film broadcast industry was at stake and the solution required a unique collaboration between and among all industry professionals to collectively and definitively determine the future financial realities of their business, the creation of solutions that will keep the business alive, and provide all parties an equitable piece of the pie.

Big Law Inequality for Women

In 2016, female partners in Big Law law firms comprised the other industry professionals who pronounced publicly that they were following the USWNT's pursuit of equal pay. As reported in the *New York Times* in late August 2017, Kerrie Campbell, a seasoned and extremely successful partner at the white-shoe, elite, so-called Big Law firm Chadbourne & Parke, filed an unprecedented lawsuit against the firm seeking more than $100 million for her and her female partner colleagues alleging that male partners prohibited women from ascending to leadership positions at the firm and that female partners—who incidentally brought in more revenue for the firm than most of the men—earned up to 40 percent less than their male counterparts.

In fact, the *Times* reported that despite bringing in upwards of $5 million dollars in revenue in 2014, Ms. Campbell was paid less than her male counterparts, received no bonus, and was placed in the bottom third of partner compensation metrics. To add insult to injury, when she questioned firm management about her comparatively low pay and no bonus despite her high revenue generation that year, she was told her 2014 revenue was a "fluke."

Sound familiar? Notably, when we challenged US Soccer's chief negotiator with the USWNT's $20 million in revenue versus the USMNT's $5 million revenue for 2014-15 fiscal year, he characterized it as an "aberration" and not a reason to equalize pay for the USWNT who at that time earned $72,000 per year to the USMNT's $290,000 per annum.

After challenging the law firm's management with regard to why male partners generating the same revenues received twice as many compensation-determining "points" than she was awarded, again, Ms. Campbell was reminded that the firm management compensation committee regarded her extraordinary 2014 revenue generation to be a fluke. Further, Ms. Campbell told the *Times* that when she asked questions and challenged the compensation structures she was "disrespected, demoted, and effectively terminated."

Subsequently, the firm dismantled the resources Ms. Campbell needed to effectively practice and service her clients, designated her practice to be incompatible with the firm, reduced her pay, and gave her until the end of August 2016 to leave the firm.

Unfortunately, Ms. Campbell's story is all too commonplace for powerful, successful women in the Big Law industry.

Disparate Workforces But Same Equal Pay Battles

"If you can see it, you can be it." But, in reality, that has not always been the case for women, especially when the *it* is an educated credentialed professional, such as a lawyer, doctor, financial services provider, pedigreed public service provider, or member of the United States Women's National Soccer Team. And just being "it" is not enough. Getting meritorious or equal compensation is the supreme objective. The mere fact that in the year 2024, more than sixty years after the passage of the Equal Pay Act, whether or not professional women will get paid at the same level as their equally qualified male counterparts is still a question is truly an abomination.

But the facts are the facts. Professional women are still underpaid. Recent surveys conclude that women are paid eighty-two cents on the dollar when compared to their male counterparts. Accordingly, if a man is paid $100,000 to be an associate at a major law firm, a comparable female associate will get paid $82,000.

Of course, the real cynics will champion the massive increase in compensation women have enjoyed since 1979 when women only earned 62.3 percent of what men earned, and that same female associate who earned $62,300 to her male counterparts $100,000 in 1979, is now making $82,000.

Progress, right?

If the typical male mantra of the US Soccer Federation was applied to this disparate income situation, professional women would be told: "Why are you women complaining? You should just be happy to be here and have a job. Now you have a job that pays you $20,000 more than it paid in 1979!"

Essentially, despite robust, seemingly never-ending discussion about equal pay since the passage of the Equal Pay Act of 1963, the actual "baby step" progress made with regard to women in the workforce actually getting paid fairly and equally has been alarming.

Since there has been incremental progress towards equal pay in the workforce, I thought it would be important to talk to women in different age groups about their professional experiences with equal pay. Obviously, this is not a scientific examination, but I thought it would be interesting to determine whether or not there is a difference between women's "equal pay experience" in the workplace of the older generation (sixty-plus) compared to the women in the younger modern generation (mid-thirties).

An environmental lawyer whom I have personally known for over forty-five years was one woman I had extensive talks with about her experience when she was working. Kay, as I will refer to her here, is now enjoying the retired life, but she had an extensive thirty-year law career, where she was a partner at two large San Francisco law firms.

Keiko is a lawyer and cryptocurrency professional in her mid-thirties. While she was just starting as a lawyer, she dealt with copious amounts of mistreatment and similar wage discrimination.

Throughout the process of talking to these women, four common themes kept coming up when they talked about their experiences dealing with discrimination. I will briefly explore each of the recurring themes that appear to comprise the all too common experiences that plague women in the workforce.

"Worth"

The intrinsic value of a woman's worth has never been on the same footing as a man, whether it be a man with more experience, the same experience, or even less. There is absolutely no debate here as history and statistics have shown this as the case.

Like Ms. Campbell at Chabourne, Kay demanded to know why certain male lawyers who billed fewer hours than her, generated less revenue than her, accrued zero professional acclaim, and did not invest countless pro bono hours earned hundreds and thousands of dollars more than her each year! Kay soldiered on for almost fifteen years until she could no longer tolerate the blatant, unapologetic inequities and unequal compensation.

She knew that some of her male counterparts who were considered "superstars" of the law firm—whether they worked hard or not—started to get paid four to five times more than she did over time. Remember, women like Kay were still as, if not more diligent than the men and brought in business on par if not exceeding that of the so-called firm male "superstars."

One of her male colleagues actually told her that his compensation was just based on what "he was worth" in the market at the time and because of his intrinsic "worth" he could walk out of that law firm and still get paid similarly at another firm. Quite frankly, he told Kay that he should be paid more than her and her female partners simply because he was simply *worth it*.

"Simply worth it" seemed to be the attitude of US Soccer board member and equal pay negotiator Donna Shalala when she matter-of-factly blurted out "merit pay" when I asked for an explanation to why the USMNT get paid more than the USWNT. For Shalala, the US Men's National Soccer Team was intrinsically worth more than the US Women's National Soccer Team.

Imagine spending decades just to get in the same room as these male lawyers, just to be told blatantly that their male counterparts were simply worth more, with no further explanation. Just like Kay, the USWNT had to maintain excellence, continue to win, and essentially build a dynasty just to get to the bargaining table with the US Soccer Federation … only to have those two words *merit pay* get uttered back as if that is a legitimate counter during negotiations.

Remember, in order to fight for what you feel like is right in compensation and plain ole respect, you must know your own worth, and not be afraid to let people know about it.

"Aberration"

In negotiations, it is not uncommon for the opposing side to use excuses when presented with statistics or other facts to challenge their position, or to objectively demonstrate your perspective and point of view, or to simply highlight the reasons why you are bringing something to their attention. Just like when the male executives at Ms. Campbell's law firm insultingly characterized her stellar 2014 revenue performance as a mere fluke. In response, she plastered her superiors with hard core facts that vilified the "fluke" demonization of her work and demolished their reasons for not paying her what she was clearly worth.

According to Kay, when a male partner had a bad year, the firm's partner compensation gurus characterized it as a "one-off," an "aberration" of sorts and despite his bad annual revenue performance, the nonperforming partner still received the same partner compensation he received in his "good" year, which was still higher than that paid to a performing female partner.

As noted earlier, the US Soccer Federation's 2014-15 financials showed the USWNT generating $20 million in revenue and an operating profit of $17 million revenue, while the USMNT posted revenue of $5 million and an operating loss of $2 million. As noted earlier, when confronted with these financial facts, Russ Sauer, US Soccer's chief negotiator, emotionally declared out loud in an official CBA negotiating session that the financial's depicting USWNT revenue vastly outpacing the USMNT's revenues was an *aberration* … a fluke, not normal and unwelcome. Sauer's outburst exemplified the lengths to which an employer will go, and the depths of untruths they are willing to embrace to make sure women are valued less than men in worth, compensation and respect.

Fear of Fighting For Equal Pay

Next is probably one of the ongoing themes that has run throughout this entire tome. Having the guts to fight for what feels right. In order to achieve equal pay, there cannot be any doubt or skepticism when pressuring your employer or they will smell it and eat you alive!

Kay, the strong woman that she is, repeatedly bought up the issue of compensation inequality that plagued the female partners of the Big Law law firm when compared to the men. Notably, the male partners heard Kay and her female colleagues, patronized them, and promised to "look into, change and make right" the unequal compensation issues.

Much to their surprise and dismay, despite the male partner's promises to change, they never did.

It is important to note that this happens quite often in the workplace. The top brass promises changes will be made, but in reality, they just hope that after some time, the female promoter of equal pay will shut up and let the issue pass with no changes. That is why it is so crucial for women to be present, persistent and keep fighting for what they believe in.

Because of the firm's inaction, during a partner meeting with the vice-chairman of the law firm, Kay and several of her female colleagues once again raised the issue about the stark disparity between what the women and male partners were paid. Kay vociferously reiterated that female partners were not paid equitably to their male counterparts. Mirroring the treatment Hope Solo received from US Soccer's leadership as she extolled the disparities in compensation, the law firm's chairman got super annoyed with Kay for bringing it up yet again. She asked him to bring in an external consultant to do the math, a partner salary audit, but he got offended and said that was ludicrous. The executives were not interested in conducting and/or discussing an objective analysis of partner compensation in the law firm.

Incredibly, just as US Soccer was willing to sacrifice the valuable public embrace of the World Cup champion USWNT by not providing equal pay, the old boys would rather absorb the loss of Kay's huge revenues and profit stream she generated than to equalize her partner compensation. Clearly, sexism, wage discrimination, and the "good old boy" system is alive and well.

Commitment to Fight for Equal Pay

Simply put, it isn't going to be smooth sailing when fighting for what you feel is your worth. Be prepared for the employer to pull all the stops, use some dubious excuses, whether legitimate or not, just to fight back and stop you from achieving your equal pay goals. It is imperative to understand that every road block is meant to be conquered, and it all leads to the end game, which in this case is equal pay.

Kay was tired of inaction from her law firm and decided to take matters into her own hands. So, like Ms. Campbell at Chadbourne, after twenty years, Kay eventually left the law firm. Why should she stay somewhere if they didn't even value her as a properly compensated human being? Accordingly, Keiko left the government sector and entered the private sector, immersed herself in cryptocurrency, established her expertise, and as an entrepreneur, established the Puerto Rico Blockchain Trade Association the mission of which is to educate and train professionals in the emerging financial world of crypto. Moreover, her cryptocurrency company employs mostly women, with the goal of empowering women to strive to be the best version of themselves.

And as Hope Solo and I have said, the USWNT were so close to achieving equal pay but ended up settling for less and not achieving it. In some instances, when you can feel momentum building on your side, it is important to not lose sight of the goal of equal pay and stay patient, and vigorously battle the urge and enticing temptation to settle for something less than equal pay when the powers put on the full-court press, challenge your sense of reason and issue that existential ultimatum.

What We Can Learn from These Inequalities

In their respective quests for equality and respect, both women, one in the private sector, the other in the public sector, with thirty-five years separating their respective experiences, encountered counterintuitive roadblocks on their respective roads to income equality. In one instance, it's the good old boy network populated by white males who grow up believing themselves to be superior, entitled, more worthy than women, and devoid of any obstacles on their road to ensure economic prosperity. On the other, professional women who for whatever reason are allowed to work alongside them are paid substantially less, perennially hope that their exemplary service and supreme revenue generation will catch the eye of the men who earn more doing the same job under the same work conditions—only to be denied equal pay—not only by the men controlling the purse strings but also by women like Shalala and RUEMMLER who sanctify and agree that the women do not deserve and are not worthy of equal pay.

In 2024, this is the unfortunate reality for women in the workforce. Real change requires professional "wins" which creates leverage, which in turn spawns the plan and the guts required to make equal pay demands. Then that evolves into commitment to seek equality, which then leads to the development of the nuclear bombs that will be needed in the battle, and then ultimately the execution of the equal pay plan.

The 2015 USWNT created the blueprint, tactics, and environment in which the equal pay plan could be deployed. Presently, as I pen these words, the 2023 Spanish Women's World Cup champions, like the 2015 USWNT World Cup champions, victims of decades of unequal treatment and compensation exacted by the Royal Spanish Soccer Federation (RFEF) are attempting to exploit their victory into the leverage they need to not only adopt the USWNT blueprint and tactics that can result in equal pay, but also the power they need right now to fight the misogyny exhibited for the world to see, with the unwanted kiss planted squarely on the lips of star player Jenni Hermoso by the Spanish federation President Luis Rubiales as the team celebrated the victory in the awards podium.

The players have proclaimed that they would not play again until Rubiales and the entire, embattled management team, including the female head coach who apparently for years harboured doubts about the federation and despite pleas for help from the team did nothing, are terminated.

Winning leads to leverage, which converts to power!

However, even in this instance, even though the Spanish federation eventually terminated the head coach, and after several weeks of defiance, Mr. Rubiales did succumb to public and the Spanish criminal justice system pressure to resign and face criminal charges for planting the unwanted kiss on Ms. Hermoso, the federation still held the ultimate "ace" card that they knew could win the war.

Specifically, the Spanish Women's World Cup champions did have a paltry but nevertheless alternate source of income. In addition to playing for the Spanish national team, most of them played for professional club soccer teams. However, in order to receive compensation from a professional team, each player had to have a license to play professionally. Importantly, the professional play licenses are issued by the Spanish federation.

Thus, when the Spanish players threatened to never again play for the Spanish National Women's Soccer Team, the federation threatened to revoke each player's professional license. Absent the license, they could not play and earn essential income from their respective professional teams.

Again, like the USWNT, when faced with the choice of continuing their courageous battle for equality or opting for financial survival, despite their professed total commitment to achieving equality, the Spanish Women's World Cup champions, like their American counterparts, elected to embrace financial survival.

Was this another lost opportunity to capture equality while the entire world looked on in support? Did the Spanish Women's World Cup Champions throw away the career sacrifices made by their 12 colleagues –players on the "A" Team of the Spain's Women's Soccer Team who elected to NOT PLAY in the 2023 World Cup in protest of the disparate treatment the Team received from the Spanish Federation? Did those Players forfeit their careers and lifelong dream of winning a World Cup in vain? The USWNT blueprint to equal pay, the watchword of success also *not* executed by the USWNT ... 100 percent commitment to the objective of equality.

The USWNT blueprint to equal pay required 100% execution on the commitment to equality and the USWNT fell short and did not fully execute. Did the World Cup Champion Spanish Women's National Soccer Team blink and, like the USWNT, squander their opportunity for equality?

13

Conclusion: What the Reader Can Take from the USWNT Experience

WHEN CARLI LLOYD'S improbable, 50-yard, ever-elevating kick over the Japanese goalkeeper's head and into the back of the net sealed the World Cup championship for the 2015 US Women's National Soccer Team, little did they or anyone else know at that time, that Lloyd's game-winning goal was the flashpoint of the modern-day equal pay revolution in women's soccer. That goal and the ensuing World Cup victory gave the USWNT the leverage it needed to make the equal pay demand on the US Soccer Federation.

Likewise, seven years later in 2023, Spain's women's national team's World Cup victory will provide this ever-oppressed team (top twelve members of which actually boycotted this World Cup to protest the disparate, abusive treatment it had long endured at the hands of its oppressive federation)the leverage and worldwide exposure it needs to more importantly follow in the tactical footsteps and mimic the blueprint for equal pay left by the USWNT and several other women's national soccer teams in their respective quests for equal pay.

There's an old tried, but true saying that those that don't learn from history, are doomed to repeat it. It's unfortunate to say, but in this instance, with regard to the future of the US Women's National Soccer Team, with their acceptance of the pay-to-play compensation system, they've already begun to repeat a sordid, pre-2016 history of misplaced trust and equal pay-related shenanigans and obfuscation with the US Soccer Federation. The composition of the 2023 US Women's National Soccer Team's World Cup roster tells you all you need to know about whether or not the "cycle" has been regenerated. Fourteen of the twenty-three women on the 2023 USWNT World Cup team roster were rookies. Their first international experience, and in one case, their first "cap" (play on the US team) was in the 2023 World Cup.

Incredible.

With several of the world's developing nations investing in and fielding vastly improved women's soccer teams, all of which have elevated their skills and level of performance over the past four years since the last World Cup, it was quite likely that those nations would in fact present some formidable competitive challenges to the power teams of the world in the early rounds of the 2023 World Cup. The elevation of the women's game worldwide will at some point severely challenge the US Women's National Soccer Team on the world level. With the World Cup defending champions' struggle to beat Vietnam in group play, and early ouster in the round of 16 against Sweden, that initial challenge may have been witnessed at the 2023 World Cup.

And with FIFA's possible investment into the developing nations' women's teams, the future for the growth in the power of women's soccer is great. But, in the United States, if the age-old cycle is regenerated and players do not spend more than four years on the USWNT before being voluntarily or involuntarily cycled off before entering more senior years of their careers, several things will happen. First, probably before the 2024 Olympics, the US Women's National Soccer Team will realize that they were bamboozled into accepting and embracing the USMNT's pay-to-play compensation system in the 2022 collective bargaining agreement as the equivalent of equal pay.

That was a mistake.

Eventually, the USWNT will realize that they've been duped by US Soccer. The team will realize that they were suckered into believing that accepting the pay-to-play compensation system—the same system that used to compensate the men—is just that—a "pay system." It's not equal pay. It is a fallacy. By June 2024 after not repeating in the 2023 World Cup, the USWNT players will begin to feel the uncertainties of not knowing when and if they'll get called-up to the USWNT to play in none, some, or all of the USWNT's minimum annual thirteen-games in the pay-to-play compensation system. The fewer games USWNT players are called-up to play, the less money the players on the US women's team will make. As a result, the meagerly compensated younger players will become *old* quick.

As players, the USWNT will realize that by ascribing to the virtual roulette wheel of the pay-to play compensation system, that US Soccer has the ultimate power to spin the wheel and determine if, when, where and with which player it will stop—if at all.

The paucity of income will become a real stark, painful reality for these young players. There's nothing more prolific than aging in your sport—coupled with growing life responsibilities and families, the lack of income, the inability to pay your bills, and the feeling that you've been used and abused by your employer.

You now have a real-life decision to make. Do you continue to live out your athletic "dream" or succumb to the realities of survival? I believe this realization will happen before the 2024 Olympic Games.

Unfortunately, the difference between these young, rapidly aging in dog years USWNT players, and the seasoned veterans on the 2015 USWNT World Cup champions, will be that they will have no basis for leverage. Unlike the 2015 team that was the catalyst for equal pay when they wielded the mighty big-stick of leverage coming off of their World Cup victory, coupled with the fact that twenty-one of the twenty-four members of the team were six-plus-year veterans, this 2024 USWNT will not have the leverage of a World Cup victory, and they will not have the leverage of an Olympic victory in 2024.

Furthermore, the women will not have the leverage created by seniority and suffering, that the 2015 team had which propelled that team to be in the best position ever to extract equal pay out of the United

States Soccer Federation. Laudably, the USWNT's equal pay journey has in fact yielded huge success for women's soccer in several countries. First and foremost, the USWNT's exhibition of supreme courage to challenge their Federation and demand equal pay set the stage for national women's soccer teams in at least eight other countries to grant equal pay to their women's national teams upon their respective teams' initial request for equality in compensation.

Importantly, as I pen these words, in the midst of bitter turmoil over equal pay and other existential issues with their federation, Spain won the 2023 Women's World Cup. Notably, the victory provides them the leverage and worldwide media scrutiny they need to pressure their federation for equal pay and the other benefits they seek. Notwithstanding the misogyny openly displayed on "live" television with the president of the Spanish federation on-the-lips kiss of the team captain on the postgame victory platform, the Spanish team can instantly be the beneficiaries of and immediately execute the USWNT's blueprint battle tactics of leverage, nuclear options, guts, commitment, and execution of their plan to acquire equal pay and across the board equality.

Unfortunately, in the short-term, when faced with the choice of immediate economic survival or staying the course and continuing to make the sacrifices and commitment required to obtain equality, like their USWNT predecessor, the Spanish world champions opted for survival. But the war for equality rages on and I'm certain the short-term lessons learned by the USWNT and the Spain's World Cup champions will one day result in equality.

Remember, equal pay is an incremental endeavor. As noted earlier, despite the USWNT's inability to score its own equal pay touchdown, their quest was a huge success. Their resolve and journey inspired and gave others the courage to stand up to their federation and demand and receive equal pay. Once again, although starting from scratch, the women on the USWNT need only look within their own recent team history, project ahead, and follow the legacy blueprint left to serve as their guide to do whatever is required to rekindle the fire for equal pay for the USWNT.

Epilogue

EXPOSED.

Unmasked.

Results.

Hope.

The true colors, tactics, and agendas of the powers that be in the business of women's soccer have been exposed.

The power brokers have been unmasked.

The courage, prowess, and resolve of the women of the "beautiful game"—unleashed by the USWNT for the world to see and embrace—has empowered the previously powerless to actively and collectively demand equality.

The results—at least ten international soccer governing bodies have adopted equal pay for their women's national teams.

And as I pen this piece, the women on the 2023 World Cup champion Spanish team wasted no time condemning the strident, defiant act of misogyny perpetrated on live international television for all the world to see with the president of the Spanish federation, Luis Rubiales planting an exuberant, unwanted kiss of the lips of Spanish World Cup champion Jenni Hermoso.

The team's pushback was immediate.

The federation's reaction was typical. "Hermoso consented" was the federation's retort.

Predictably, Hermoso was pressured to support the federation's characterization of the Rubiales kiss as consensual exuberance.

But—with the power of the USWNT's legacy, and like the ten national teams that followed the American's lead—Hermoso and her teammates leveraged their day-old World Cup victory and uncharacteristically dropped a nuclear bomb and pushed back hard, defied the federation's typical intimidation tactics, and vociferously denied that the kiss was consensual, vowing to boycott games until Rubiales was fired.

In this situation, the Spanish federation's behavior was typical and expected. In fact, their initial unwavering support for Rubiales was almost cavalier, sort of matter-of-fact.

But the team's response was anything but typical.

Hopefully, despite the short-term outcome, the team's sincere and immediate exhibition of unity and genuine outrage at the all-to-common misogynistic, degrading, disrespectful actions of the Spanish federation will deter similar behavior in the future.

What's right is right, and what's wrong must change.

Progress to equality is incremental, but who said the incremental steps have to be small?

Big steps are required.

And the Spanish World Cup champions have executed and taken a big step.

Unanimity.

Leverage. Guts. Nuclear Bombs. Commitment.

Execution.

Acknowledgments

First and foremost, with great humility, I'd like to acknowledge and thank my amazing wife Jennie and my now adult children Savannah and Elliot for all of their love and unwavering support as I navigated the enormously stressful and exceedingly treacherous and choppy waters in my representation of the World Cup Champion United States Women's National Soccer Team (USWNT) and the pursuit of equal pay that at times, absent family presence, support, and comfort, would have consumed me.

Next, I'd like to acknowledge and bestow on all of the authors out there my deepest sense of respect. Writing a book is one of the most difficult things I've ever done. And I've been involved in some very difficult situations.

And as all authors know, no author writes a book alone.

Thus, at this time, I'd like to acknowledge all of those who provided me overt, covert, silent, aggressive and passive aggressive support, from the time in 2018 when I first contemplated writing this book and then, after I took the plunge.

Over what seemed like an eternity but was truly just about one (1) year, I suffered through what seemed like thousands of drafts of the book proposal until finally getting it right, submitting it to would-be publishers, and hitting paydirt with Skyhorse Publishing.

Thank you to Skyhorse Publishing and my fabulous, exceedingly mellow and proficient editor Julie Perry for believing in this project.

Further, I'd like to thank my pugnacious and sweet literary agent, Nena Madonia of The Nominate Group. I've known Nena for 15 years. Nena is a no nonsense, super energized, confident, effervescent person who can fire you up at a moment's notice. More importantly, she is brutally truthful and provides sometimes cold and painful, but always honest truths about your writing.

In a word, she makes you better.

And I appreciate that Nena was the one who convinced me—against my pretty aggressive aversion—that I needed a writer to work with me to transform my legalese into prose that could be absorbed, digested, understood, and enjoyed by readers.

Nena found Sam Yip.

And Sam was kind of a godsend.

Sam was involved in the first edit of whatever I wrote and, as a writer, has the innate capacity to inject nuance in the right spots, add words that transition from one granular start to another, and provided much needed guidance, confidence, support, solace, and direction for me at times when as a new author, deep into the weeds of writing the manuscript, I sometimes lost my sense of direction.

So, many thanks to Sam .

Next to acknowledge and thank is the cool, calm, smart, always level-headed, and disarming, but ready at a moment's notice to defend with a lion-like ferocity is Arthur McAfee.

Art has been with me for the entire ten (10) year journey in representation of and association with the United States Women's National Soccer Team. In late 2014, Art was my first call after I agreed to represent the USWNT. I told him I didn't have any money to pay him, but in the ensuing battle for equal pay, the USWNT needed his decades of in-the-trenches experience and expertise as former Senior Counsel to the NFL Players Association with regard to successfully negotiating ground-breaking, high-compensation yielding collective bargaining agreements for NFL players.

Without hesitation Art said: "I'm in".

And he has been my go-to-guy over the years as I struggled with making the decision about whether or not I wanted to revisit the often times gut wrenching emotional USWNT equal pay journey that would be required to write this book. Art was, is, and remains encouraging and supportive.

Even though the machinations of Hope Solo's equal pay litigation against US Soccer is not widely covered in this book, I would be totally remiss if I did not acknowledge and thank the incredible, diverse in personage, expertise, motivations, commitment and the decidedly delicious aplomb of my talented legal team each of whom joined me without getting paid to represent Hope Solo in her historic, first of its kind federal lawsuit against US Soccer for violation of the Equal Pay Act and Title VII wage discrimination. In March 2019, the USWNT eventually followed Hope's lead and separately filed an equal pay class action lawsuit against the Federation that essentially mirrored Hope's lawsuit.

Accordingly, first up and in without any hesitation was the talented and seasoned California employment lawyer Timothy Moppin. Working with a less than forty-eight (48) hour lawsuit filing deadline, Tim stepped up to the plate and joined me to draft and timely submit Hope's federal equal pay lawsuit in August 2018.

Additionally, Paul Stafford, my former law partner and great litigator from Dallas was always on the ready to step in when needed to draft emergency motions, provide "on the run" advice and counsel or jump on a flight to California to interview a witness or make a court appearance.

Next, the indefatigable A.J. De Bartolomeo.

A.J. and her law partner Ariana J. Tadler joined our legal team as our class action law experts. Despite vociferous battles between and amongst us, A.J. provided a fierce, take-no-prisoners, timely and absolutely expert advice and counsel approach with regard to the USWNT's class action lawsuit against US Soccer, how that case impacted Hope's equal pay case against the Federation, and how we needed to position and reposition Hope's litigation against US Soccer in federal court.

And the last but certainly not the least to join Hope's legal team, big-time kudos to Jim Trusty, former Chief of the United States Department of Justice Organized Crime & Gang Section and RICO expert who joined in 2020 to help us consider and pursue our theories and potential RICO claims against US Soccer in pursuit of equal pay.

Finally, the ultimate acknowledgment and thanks to the one person who was "all in," and unlike her teammates, demonstrated total commitment to equal pay, and as a result, lost her spot on the USWNT and ultimately forfeited her career —the GOAT goalkeeper Hope Solo.